VERDICT

THE JURY SYSTEM

VERDICT

THE JURY SYSTEM

Morris J. Bloomstein

REVISED EDITION

DODD, MEAD & COMPANY
NEW YORK

347.7
B

ISBN: 0-396-06608-9
Library of Congress Catalog Card Number: 72-1537
Printed in the United States of America
by The Cornwall Press, Inc., Cornwall, N.Y.

To my most sympathetic jury, my parents

Contents

1 Roots of the System

THE BUZZER SOUNDS. The bleak courtroom, bare a moment
ago, now rapidly fills with people scurrying in from the
corridor. There are the lawyers, relatives and friends of
the accused, perhaps others who are interested in the outcome of the case, all now suddenly alert. The buzzer, con-
nected to the courtroom from the jury deliberation room,
sounds again.

Verdict.

The jury has reached a verdict.

All are in place now, including the judge on his bench,
and the courtroom attendant leads the twelve men to their
seats in the jury box. For days they had sat there, expres-
sionless, perhaps listening, perhaps not. There is no way
of telling.

As the time to speak nears, the jurors, void of expression
to the end, stare straight ahead, glancing neither at the
prosecutor nor at the defendant and his lawyer.

The foreman rises.

"Mister Foreman, has the jury reached a verdict?," asks
the judge.

"It has, your Honor."

"How does the jury find?"

There is a pause while the jurors' eyes, as if on signal, rise to the defendant's. It is a never-ending split second.

"Not guilty."

It is over and time flows normally once again. The jury has spoken.

Who are these twelve Gods with the power of life and death? From whence came a handful of strangers to decide another's future?

This is the jury and this is its story.

Juries are used today to decide a multiplicity of questions. Criminal cases are the first thing that come to mind, but this is not all. Lawsuits over contracts, accident cases, claimed debts, hearings to determine sanity—all these and many more issues may be tried before juries. Name the problem and it has probably been tried before a jury somewhere, sometime.

Trial by jury is now so widespread that we take it for granted, as much a feature of our everyday life as the supermarket. There was a time, however, when there were no juries. It was an undreamed-of concept. Where did it start?

The birth of the first rudimentary jury system was in relatively ancient times, arising in olden Greece. Yet prior to that time, the world had flourished without it. The countries of the Orient had no such system. Among the very ancient Western cultures, such as the Jews and Phoenicians, no jury was to be found. In these two civilizations, disputes were often decided by the priests, who made their rulings, not according to what had been decided in previous cases, as in our present system of law, but according to how they felt in that particular case. (Among the Jews, butchers could not be used to dispense justice because the necessary forbearance or compassion for blood or pain could not be expected from them. Centuries later, the English used the same rationale in their method of jury selection, excluding persons in certain occupations.)

Another non-jury empire was ancient Egypt, where decisions were made by a president and thirty associates (ten from each of the great cities of Heliopolis, Thebes, and Memphis). All procedures were carried out in writing. No oral arguments by trial lawyers were permitted since, as one legal writer of the period put it, "By their exclusion, the clever and tricky had no undue advantage over the simple and honest, as they could not avail themselves of rhetorical flourishes and appeals to the passions."

As Greece was the cradle of liberty, so was it the place of origin of the jury system, or, at least, the forerunner of it. The key to the Greek system was the use of *dikasteries*. Well before the time of the birth of Christ, the Greeks selected by lot six thousand citizens (thereafter called *dikasts*) above thirty years of age and divided into smaller groups, called *decuries*. When a civil or criminal trial was ready to be held, lots were drawn to determine in which *decury* and court the case was to be heard, so that no one could know in advance before whom the case would appear and attempt to influence the decision.

"Juries" were large at this time. During the era of Pericles (467-428 B.C.) the *decury* consisted of between two hundred and five hundred *dikasts,* and sometimes, in important trials, a thousand, fifteen hundred, or even two thousand members. By the very size of such *decuries,* corruption, bribery, and intimidation were rendered highly improbable.

However, there were serious drawbacks. Imagine the mob scene that developed when such a swollen, oversized group had to decide important questions of property and even of life or death. In addition, the citizens who served on the *decuries* received as pay half a *drachma,* or nine cents. Even allowing for greater purchasing power at that time, this was small recompense, indeed. Still, in those days of vast unemployment, this was sufficient money for the over-aged and the poor to fight to obtain. As a result, these classes, in practice, largely constituted the "juries."

In criminal trials, those who were convicted and fined paid the money to the state. Since a large percentage of such money was expended on public galas and shows, a tremendous temptation was laid on the less privileged classes serving as jurors (*dikasts*) to find everyone guilty, especially rich defendants. These "juries," composed in large part of the uneducated, unemployed, and resentful elements of the populace, were quick to vent their spleen on those who were better off than they.

Socrates, under accusation, spoke in such lofty tones—"If I am to receive my deserts, I ought to have the highest honors paid me . . ."—that the enraged *dikasts* immediately condemned him to death.

So there were faults in the system. Call it controlled mob rule, law by the least reasoning and responsible of the populace. Call it unwieldy, if not unworkable. But . . , it was the first. Here, at this point in history, the finger is pointed at the earliest system that embodied the basic principles of the jury as we know it.

The second great society to use a form of the jury was, inevitably, the Romans. As to civil suits—that is, those claims by one individual against another, not involving a crime—the Roman system was broken into two parts. The issues of the dispute were defined by a judge. The decision as to how to dispose of the issues was referred to one or more private persons, known as a *judex*, or, in the plural, *judices*. These private persons corresponded roughly to our juries.

The exact method of choosing *judices* (jurors) is not known, but suggestions have been made by authorities on the history of the law. Sometimes the parties themselves agreed to specific *judices*, or a list of selected persons was submitted to the parties and undesirable names were struck from the roll.

How did the *judices* operate? Unlike today's trials, there was no judge to preside at the hearing, to determine which witnesses were competent to testify, which evidence was admissible, what previous decisions had been made on similar sets of facts, or, indeed, what the law was. To remedy this, each jury, or set of *judices*, had one lawyer on it to attempt to set guidelines. This was not a lawyer as we know the term, but a man with some legal knowledge. There were methods whereby objections could be made to *judices* if they were too close to the parties or otherwise involved and apt to be prejudiced.

Judices were supreme—and the law was vicious. If the defendant had been required to pay a certain amount and did not do so within thirty days (or if no one would guarantee payment) his body was forfeited to the plaintiff, the person bringing suit. The defendant, after certain ceremonies (such as chaining the defendant for sixty days in the plaintiff's house and announcing his debts three times in the market place) could be sold into slavery, or be killed and his body divided up among his creditors. In fact, the law stated, "On the third market day let him be cut into pieces; if anyone cut too much or too little, it will not be a crime." Imagine that being done today because someone didn't pay his grocery bill.

In criminal cases, in the very early days of Rome, trials took place before the entire populace, except for high treason, which was tried before the Senate. Soon, as crime and population mounted, this practice became unworkable. There grew up a system of trials before a *quaestor*, or magistrate, and a group of *judices*. Ignoring the names that sound strange to us today, what you had was a hearing before a judge and a jury—a modern trial.

There was just one problem. The juries became too powerful and independent for imperial power to control. The Emperor, therefore, abolished the system in A.D. 352. From then on, judges alone made the decisions, presumably judges appointed by the Emperor.

In the early-day Germany of scattered tribes, the lord of the territory had one hundred co-assessors, men of the village, sitting with him as judges. They decided what the custom of the community was and how it applied to the case at hand.

Later, the head of the court (called the Graf, or Count) had a small group of landholders, known as freemen, to help him. Usually seven in number, the "jurors" were quite often increased to twelve in important cases. When a decision was to be made, they retired out of the Graf's presence so they could speak freely, a custom found today in the seclusion of our own juries behind closed doors while deliberating. It was not easy to be such a juror, however, since these seven might themselves be challenged to a fight by the loser and six of his friends.

The jury system spread across the face of Europe as wanderers carried the idea from group to group. More than a thousand years ago it was found in Scandinavia, and even at that time it was referred to as an ancient institution. Norway had a system whereby three officials named persons from each district to attend the court, or "Thing," as it was called. From the total number chosen, thirty-six persons were selected to act in a capacity much like a jury. They were presided over by a *Loegmann*, or lawman, whose sole qualification was that he could recite the laws of the land from memory. The laws were quite simple at this time, and were more like rules of fair play. The jurors had the right not only to decide the issues but, if the defendant were found guilty, the sentence as well. If the thirty-six agreed unanimously, the decision was final; if not, the lawman could decide. Then, too, the king could overrule the lawman.

Thus read the oath the Norse jurors took:

> I protest before God that I will give such a vote in every cause, as well on the side of plaintiff as defendant, as I consider most just in the sight of God, according to law and my conscience, and I shall always do the same, whenever I shall be chosen as juror.

Sweden had juries of twelve. Agreement of a majority of the jury—seven—was sufficient to decide the case.

Denmark missed out on the opportunity of introducing the jury system into England. At first, the Danes also had "Things." Seven jurors were a quorum at a Thing, although in some complicated cases, the number reached twenty-four. Following this system, juries of twelve came into vogue, chosen by the people in the district, a magistrate or the prosecutor. The majority ruled, but their decision was not really final. A bishop and eight men of the district could review and reverse the decision. The missed opportunity occurred when King Canute, the man who ordered the tide to stop merely to show his courtiers that a ruler was not all-powerful, became ruler of England in 1014. He never attempted to incorporate the jury system into his newly-won land.

We think of Iceland today as a backwater area, somewhere up in the cold portion of the globe. It was at one time, however, a haven for Norwegian aristocrats who fled a political revolution in their home country, bringing the basic jury principle with them. "Things" were carried one step further in Iceland. The local Things, called Varthings, were directly responsible to a central Thing, established in A.D. 928, and called, rather grandiosely, the Althing, or Universal Thing. A code of procedure was used, called "The Grey Goose." The number of jurors varied from five, nine or twelve, depending upon the case.

Somewhat similar to today's qualifications for jurors, the Icelanders required their jurors to be twenty years of age, of no close relationship to the parties, in good health, and from the district where the incident had occurred. As would be expected, however, in a society founded by the "aristocrats" of that day, only those from the higher classes of society were chosen.

Rollo, the Scandinavian, led his people into Normandy, in what is today France, about the year A.D. 890. Ravaging, pillaging, as any self-respecting Norse raider would do, he brought and left an unexpected by-product, the jury system that had been in use in his homeland. Quickly taking root in Normandy, it was refined and altered, awaiting its time of transplantation.

When William the Conqueror crossed the English Channel and conquered the English in A.D. 1066, the invisible passenger on board his ships was the jury system.

2 Unmerrie Olde England

ENGLISH LAW IS THOUGHT of today by some people as peculiarly English, unique. It is regarded as pure, untainted by foreign influence, springing from time immemorial out of the passion for justice of a united people.

Nothing could be further from the truth.

Norsemen, Romans, Picts, Scots, Angles, Saxons, and Normans all came to the island, conquering, yet leaving part of themselves, as a rushing wave will leave new sand on the shore. Part of what they left was the dispute-deciding technique that had evolved within each group, what in a more sophisticated society would be called "the Law."

When Caesar invaded Britain in 55 B.C., his administrator, C. Julius Agricola, introduced Roman law. Although the Roman legal influence lasted in Britain, the Romans themselves didn't. In A.D. 448, the last legions withdrew.

The ancient Britons who remained found themselves fighting the Picts and Scots. Having become used to the support of Roman arms, the Britons were soon inundated by invaders. Thus, the mistake was made of "calling in the wolves to protect the islanders from the foxes." The new "allies," the Angles and Saxons, Germanic-descended mainlanders, arrived in England, defeated the Picts and Scots, and then turned conquerors.

These tribes, more easily described as Anglo-Saxons, had very little in the way of a legal system to impart to their new domains. A bounty granted to the Church atoned for every act of violence against Society.

No overall juridical organization was present in Britain until the reign of King Alfred (871-901), he of the burnt cakes and other legends. Upon acceding to the throne he divided all England into counties, the counties into hundreds, and the hundreds into tithings. Ten neighboring householders formed one tithing, every householder answering for the conduct of his family. Ten tithings formed a hundred. Any man who did not register with one tithing or another was punished as an outlaw. The system resulted in making everyone responsible to someone.

When conflicts arose, as they must, the entire tithing met and decided the issue. Here, in a rough, ill-lit room, suffused with the smell of unwashed illiterates, justice was dispensed. An appeal of sorts could even be had to the hundred—representatives of the tithings under its sway— which met once every four weeks. To decide on the questions raised before it, twelve freeholders were chosen from the hundred. Presided over by what then posed as a judge, the freeholders swore to administer impartial justice.

Following the death of Alfred, incessant warfare and the emerging customs of the people caused the Alfredian structure to decay and alter. Gradually, there arose a system called compurgation, or oath-taking, which was destined, in altered form, to play a large part in the development of trial by jury. Brought in by the Saxons and at first limited to criminal matters, it was subsequently extended to all matters.

To what did these compurgators swear? They were certainly not witnesses, for they might know nothing of the facts in dispute. They were not jurors, for no evidence was submitted to them. They were merely friends of the party who summoned them. By their united oaths, the compurgators, usually twelve in number, swore that they knew their friend to be a truthful and honest man and that they believed in the justness of his cause.

At a later time, when it was plain to be seen by even the relatively uncivilized inhabitants of the Britain of that day that not everyone was telling the truth, the whole truth, and nothing but the truth, there were appointments made in each district of sworn witnesses whose duty it was to attend all sales, execution of charters, and the like. They were not subject to cross-examination, and their oaths were decisive in case of dispute. Later, persons qualified by circumstances, though not preappointed, could similarly testify to prove age, ownership of chattels, and other cut-and-dried factual matters.

For the ordinary civil dispute, however, the assertions of a party in his own favor were admitted as conclusive, provided compurgators, usually twelve in number, supported the party. It was at this point that the "game" began. The party's opponent could produce a greater number of compurgators to prove *his* case, and then the original party could produce more friends, and the opponent . . . ad infinitum. In one case it is reported that a person by the name of Ulnothus produced a thousand witnesses to prove title to an estate!

The general rule of that day was that witnesses were counted instead of the quality of their testimony being weighed. Of course, if the number of compurgators on each side was about equal, the relative ranks of the witnesses were taken into account.

In criminal cases, if the compurgators agreed (and the defendant wasn't caught in the act), there was a complete acquittal. If, however, the accused could not present a proper number of oath-takers, had previously been accused of larceny or perjury, or if for some other reason he was thought unworthy of belief, he was required to undergo the Ordeal.

Though the Ordeal was, in effect, an appeal to the protection of Heaven, it was accompanied by the customary cruelty and savagery encountered in everyday English life of the time.

In trial by Ordeal, the methods usually used were hot irons, hot water, and cold water. The hot and cold water tests were used for the common folk, while the hot iron method was reserved for the nobility.

If the accused was required to undergo the Ordeal by hot water, he put his head or whole arm into it, depending on the degree of the offense. If the Ordeal was by cold water, his thumbs were tied to his toes and he was thrown into a river or lake. If he escaped unharmed by the boiling water or if he sank in the cold water, he was declared innocent. If he was hurt by the boiling water or if he floated in the river, he was guilty.

In the case of Ordeal by the hot iron, the accused's hand was first sprinkled with holy water. A red-hot iron, one to three pounds in weight, was placed in his hand and he was required to take nine paces. At the ninth step, he threw down the iron and hastened to the altar where his hand was bound. After three days his hand was unbound. If it had healed, he was innocent; if not, guilty.

Various other methods of Ordeal were used, some less physically punishing. The Decision by the Cross was one. Two pieces of wood were laid on an altar, one marked with a cross. After prayer for a sign from God, a priest or some inexperienced youth would pick up one of the sticks without looking. If it was the stick that bore the cross, the defendant was innocent. If it was the unmarked stick, he was guilty.

Then there was the Ordeal of the Accursed Morsel. A piece of bread was prayed over, that it might choke the defendant if he were guilty. Then it was swallowed. In light of the superstition that prevailed during those years, it cannot come as much of a shock that many men did choke to death, including Godwin, Earl of Kent and father of Harold, last Saxon king of England. This test, however, was reserved almost exclusively for the clergy.

The priests of that time were in charge of administering most of these tests of innocence, and it was open and notorious that a rich harvest was reaped from the privilege, depending upon the wealth and guilt of the accused.

Trial by Ordeal lingered into the thirteenth century, and seems to have been the final basis for decision when an accused person was too old or was disabled and could not venture into trial by battle—that is, personal combat between the opposing parties—or when compurgators or witnesses could not be found or were contradictory.

In the middle of the eleventh century the Normans came.

The Normans left more untouched than they changed. They adopted the use of the local Anglo-Saxon courts, appeals to the King, the use of legal witnesses, compurgation, and the Ordeal.

However, certain changes were made. The spiritual and temporal courts were separated, thus curtailing the influence of the clergy in the day-to-day work of the judicial system. Circuit judges were appointed by the King. Traveling throughout the realm, they dispensed the King's justice, as opposed to the "hundred" or county court.

With the same sense of justice as those who instituted the Ordeal, the Normans introduced trial by combat. The parties, or more usually, champions designated by the parties, dueled and judgment was entered for that party whose champion had prevailed. Quite in keeping with such logic, the vanquished champion was punished for having borne false witness. Variations of the system permitted the party to challenge not only his adversary, but the witnesses or the judge himself.

No defense can be made for this system except that it provided the ultimate expedient to obtain a decision. It was partly based on the idea that where legal measures had failed, recourse must be made to the law of force.

Actually, the Normans also brought to England the inquest and inquisition to determine facts. Consisting of persons representing a number of townships, they were convened and presided over by a judge or other representative of the Crown and, more importantly, were selected for their knowledge of the facts in the particular case at hand. They decided the dispute, rarely hearing evidence from other witnesses.

At the same time, there appeared accusatory tribunals whose duty it was to charge offenders and put them on trial before a judge. Here was the beginning of the grand jury. There was no fixed number of members, it depending on the local usage, although the number was usually twelve or more.

From these Norman-English foundations, there sprang the assise, an almost direct forerunner of our modern jury, although with significant distinctions. In cases where trial by combat was inapplicable, impracticable, not customary, or interdicted by the clergy, and in cases that were, at first, of generally inferior importance, men of the neighborhood where the offense was surmised to have been committed were gathered in an inquest. Those who were selected were supposed to have knowledge of the facts of the matter. Significantly, as today, friends, enemies, and near relations of the accused were excluded.

These quasi-jurors were called recognitors. The recognitor system soon came to be used in civil cases as well. The recognitors were generally twelve in number, or some multiple thereof.

During the reign of Henry II, trial by jury became somewhat general, primarily in actions involving land and related matters. The persons whose possession of land was impugned or the defendant in a matter related to such possession could make a choice between trial by battle or a trial before twelve recognitors.

Out of these recognitions arose the entire system of trial by jury as we know it. The jurors, or recognitors, were at first witnesses of the fact. In the reign of Edward I, additional persons were added to the jury. Slowly, the jurors having knowledge were separated from the other jurors and became the witnesses, leaving the decision in the hands of those not having knowledge of the facts. This latter development began in the reign of Edward III, about A.D. 1350.

Life was not easy for jurors in that day and age. There are records of juries that were shut up without food or drink until they reached a verdict. In addition, there were very few lawyers to explain fine points of law to them. In 1300, Parliament authorized the naming of forty lawyers, this number being deemed sufficient to take care of all England. These forty were primarily used by the public in disputes involving their respective claims to land.

The worst danger to the juror was attaint. If authorities decided that a jury had reached an improper decision, they could convene a second jury which would convict the first jury of having rendered a false verdict. This was held to imply perjury on the part of the original jurors (recognitors), rendering them subject to forfeiture of their lands and liberty. The attaint originated about 1200, when the jurors were witnesses, and so the basis for attaint is not so shocking. Today, we still punish witnesses who testify falsely as perjurors.

What is amazing, however, is that attaint was still applicable to juries up to 1670. At that time, two men who were being persecuted for their religious beliefs were brought to trial for unlawfully congregating with their co-religionists. Under the English statutes then prevailing, there was not a doubt that they were guilty, but with a sense of rebellion against the harshness of the law, the jury found the men not guilty. The entire jury was immediately held by the trial judge to be guilty of attaint. Riots erupted throughout England. Finally, on appeal, the entire concept of attaint was struck down. One of the two defendants was William Penn, founder of Pennsylvania.

In that same case it was held that where a juror had knowledge of facts material to a case, he must inform the court and be sworn as a witness. Finally, Lord Ellenborough, in 1816, decided that a judge who tolerated a verdict based on facts not brought out by the evidence, but founded on the jury's own peculiar knowledge, was wrong.

As to the development of the jury in criminal cases, Richard I, in the year 1194, provided for twelve knights in the county or shire to accuse and try the criminal offenders, thereby combining the functions of a grand jury (accusatory) and a petit jury (triers of the facts). Thus was compurgation nudged aside. By the act of the Lateran

Council of 1215 the Ordeal was abolished and the two juries were split apart. By the end of the thirteenth century, trial by jury in criminal cases had become common.

Curiously enough, an exception to the right of trial by jury existed in cases of secret poisoning, where the accused was obliged to defend himself by combat, because, as was said, "the country can know nothing of the fact," and recognitors with knowledge would be impossible.

Soon an even more curious development took place. Instead of a right to trial by jury, it was held that a jury trial was required in all criminal cases, even though the defendant didn't want one (due to his bad reputation in the community or the terrible nature of the crime). In fact, in the thirteenth century, if a defendant refused to be tried by a jury, it was deemed that he had confessed his guilt. Almost as bad was standing mute when asked to plead to a crime or to submit to a trial by jury.

As one British observer of the 18th century noted:

> The English judgment of penance for standing mute was as follows: that the prisoner be remanded to the prison from whence he came; and put in a low, dark chamber; and there be laid on his back, on the bare floor, naked, unless where decency forbids; that there be placed upon his body as great a weight of iron as he could bear, and more; that he have no sustenance, save (on alternate days) . . . three morsels of the worst bread and . . . three draughts of standing water . . . and in this situation the person should remain till he died or till he answered.

Why did prisoners, guilty and innocent alike, stand mute? If they were found guilty in any other than the normal manner (before a judge and jury) or if they died before trial, their lands and goods were not forfeit to the Crown. Hence, they saved what little they could for their families at the cost of their own lives. Over the years, the courts gradually discontinued this practice and, in 1827, it was abolished.

In reviewing these English centuries, there is no doubt that the roots of the modern jury were crude and cruel, consonant with the times, but from it sprang English jurisprudence and fair play, the system that spanned the Atlantic and formed the basis of our own ideal of justice.

3 The Jury Crosses the Atlantic

WHEN THE ENGLISH COLONISTS arrived in the New World, they brought part of their homeland with them. The British way of thinking and acting remained basically the same, albeit modified by circumstances and the wild and primitive nature of the new country. Retention of the old English institutions was one way of preserving a base of security in the midst of Indians and strange forests.

The jury was one of the institutions preserved. In each colony, the administration of justice became an important facet in the life of the community, although circumstances sometimes necessitated variations. In western Massachusetts in 1638, twelve fit men could not be found to serve on a jury (the rest being either working, ill, or needed for defense), and it was agreed by the colonists that juries of six would be sufficient to serve on minor matters, such as debt involving small amounts of money and similar disputes. The shortage of men was so acute that the traditional distinction between grand juries (those that ac-

cused) and petit juries (those that tried cases) could not
be maintained and the petit juror had to double as grand
juror.

The colonies in America were not started all at once. It
took 125 years for all of the charters from the various
kings that reigned during that period to be issued. Under
the circumstances, it can well be imagined that different
powers were assigned to the various founders of the colonies. In Connecticut and Rhode Island, the charters were
broad and so was the colonists' right to govern themselves,
except in certain instances that would affect the mother
country, England. In Pennsylvania and Maryland, virtually dictatorial rights had been granted to the founders
of these colonies and, unless a seldom-used royal veto was
imposed, the rulers here were the absolute masters.

For various reasons, certain colonies had no charters, or
the charter had expired or had been forfeited. New York,
New Hampshire, Carolina, Virginia, Massachusetts, Georgia, and parts of Delaware and New Jersey became royal
provinces, administered by Crown-appointed officials and
assemblies elected by the colonial landholders. The English system was used in these courts, and juries were used
in both civil and criminal trials.

As in the time of the Romans, the King and his ministers
were not always happy with the way the colonials on the
juries administered the King's laws. Quite often they found
in favor of colonist defendants on clear-cut violations of
England's statutes regarding the colonies—laws which
were deemed oppressive by the inhabitants of the new
land.

In 1734, John Peter Zenger, a newspaper publisher in New York City, published constant criticism of the then royal governor, William Cosby, an act in violation of the criminal libel laws of the time. Placed on trial before a jury of colonists and a government-appointed judge, he interposed the only possible defense, freedom of the press.

Judge De Lancy, haughtily gazing down at the jury box full of "rustics" who were to his mind something less than Englishmen, directed them to decide only if the statements about Governor Cosby had been printed by Zenger and, if so, *he* would decide if they were libelous.

Defying the judge, the jury brought in a verdict of "not guilty." Not only was this a blow for freedom of the press, it also firmly asserted the independence of the jury.

The claim of the colonists to the common-law rights of all Englishmen, which they considered themselves to be at the time, became one of universal concern. In October of 1765, delegates from nine colonies convened in New York and published a Declaration of Rights which they considered all colonists entitled to. Of particular importance was the power to tax themselves and the right to trial by jury.

Another factor that fortified American determination to hold on to the right to a jury was a work produced by an Englishman, William B. Blackstone, a judge of the Court of Common Pleas in England. Before his literary arrival upon the scene, there was no real collation of the common law of England. Research had to be done through dusty tomes to find precedents, that is, previous decisions on cases involving substantially the same principles that would now be binding on the case at hand. There was no equivalent of a legal encyclopedia to discover what the consensus of the cases said about the law on a particular subject.

In 1765, Blackstone commenced publishing his *Commentaries on the Common Law*. Becoming a "runaway best-seller" in England, and, more important for our purposes, a "must" book in America, his compilation of the common law served as the basis for the molding and influencing of the colonists' attitudes toward the law.

As to juries, Blackstone said:

> But in settling and adjusting a question of fact, when entrusted to any single magistrate, partiality and injustice have an ample field to range in . . . Here, therefore, a competent number of sensible and upright jurymen, chosen by lot from among those of the middle rank, will be found the best investigators of truth, and the surest guardians of public justice. For the most powerful individuals in the state will be cautious of committing any flagrant invasion of another's right, when he knows that the fact of his oppression must be examined and decided by twelve indifferent men, not appointed until the hour of trial; and that, when once the fact is ascertained, the law must of course redress it. This, therefore, preserves in the hands of the people that share which they ought to have in the administration of public justice, and prevents the encroachments of the more powerful and wealthy citizens.

The First Continental Congress, convening in October of 1774, declared:

That the respective colonies were entitled to the common law of England, and more especially the great and inestimable privilege of being tried by their peers of the vicinage [neighborhood], according to the course of that law; that they were entitled to the benefit of such of the English statutes as existed at the time of their colonization and which they had by experience found to be applicable to their several local and other circumstances; that they were likewise entitled to all the immunities and privileges granted and confirmed to them by royal charter, or secured by their several codes of provincial laws.

The attempt of England-appointed judges to dominate American juries so rankled the colonists that they included two specific complaints in the Declaration of Independence:

"He has made judges dependent on his Will alone, for the tenure of their offices, and the amount and payment of their salaries."

"For depriving us in many cases of the benefits of trial by jury."

It was some time after the Revolution that a Federal Constitution as we know it was approved. Prior to the enactment of the Constitution, the states had agreed to Articles of Confederation, which did not mention jury trials at all. In the meantime, most of the new states created state constitutions which, in one form or another, all guaranteed trial by jury.

Considering the fact that trial by jury was so important to the colonists it is surprising that the original Federal Constitution made no provision for trial by jury in civil cases, or for a grand jury. It only provided, in Article III, Section 2, for jury trials in criminal trials in Federal court cases. There were immediate attacks on this limited provision, the foremost of the critics being Thomas Jefferson and Patrick Henry.

Alexander Hamilton attempted to answer them in one of his Federalist Papers. He laughed at the assertion that, because the draft of the Constitution made reference to juries in criminal trials only, by inference it might be construed that juries in civil cases would be abolished. He stated that since all of the states had, as part of their institutions, juries in civil actions, the civil jury's status would be unaffected by passage of the Federal Constitution. He further pointed out that the states themselves differed on the scope of the right to jury and that it would be impossible to draw up one plan for a jury system that would reconcile the differences.

Despite Hamilton's efforts, ten amendments, becoming known as the Bill of Rights, were added to the Constitution, and the Fifth, Sixth, and Seventh spelled out in sufficient detail the right to a jury in Federal courts.

The Fifth Amendment provides, in part:

> No person shall be held to answer for a capitol, or other infamous crime unless on a presentment or indictment of a Grand Jury, except in cases arising in the land or naval forces, or in the militia, when in actual service in time of war or public danger . . .

The Sixth Amendment provides, in part:

In all criminal prosecutions, the accused shall enjoy the right to a speedy and public trial, by an impartial jury of the State and district wherein the crime shall have been committed . . .

The above two amendments apply to criminal cases. The Seventh Amendment to the Constitution applies to civil cases, and reads:

In suits at common law, where the value in controversy shall exceed twenty dollars, the right of trial by jury shall be preserved, and no fact tried by a jury shall be otherwise re-examined in any court of the United States, than according to the rules of the common law.

Let it be stated again that these particular amendments apply to Federal courts only, not to state courts. In addition, these rights do not apply to minor crimes where there is no provision for trial by jury under the old common law of England.

Much later, when it was seen that some control must be maintained over the legal actions of the individual states, the Fourteenth Amendment was added to the Constitution of the United States. It provides, in part:

Nor shall any State deprive any person of life, liberty, or property without due process of law . . .

The words "due process" are the key words here. They have been construed to mean the law and usage in England before the American Revolution and in America subsequently. This includes the right to a jury trial in a state court, although not necessarily the right to have a grand jury decide on an indictment.

As land and new territories were acquired, greatly increasing the size of this nation, Congress exercised dominion over the new tracts. Governors were appointed in each area, who then set up a Supreme Court for the territory and various district courts. Juries went hand-in-hand with the new courts—common-law juries, twelve in number, with unanimity of verdict required.

The Ordinance for the Government of the Northwest Territory, enacted in 1787, provided in Article II:

> The inhabitants of said territory shall always be entitled to the benefits of the writ of habeas corpus and trial by jury.

As each territory was admitted as a state, it acquired all the rights of the original thirteen states. Each state drew up a Constitution, in one form or another and each guaranteed the right to trial by jury. The only state that did not was Louisiana, and it provided for this by legislation. (Louisiana did not have this English heritage of the jury system, it having been governed by France before it was acquired by the United States.)

The specifics of trial by jury, of course, varied from state to state. Sometimes the particular provisions were amusing. At one time Pennsylvania had a rule that the defendant had to pay for the maintenance of the jury during its deliberations or, if he was too poor, the county would pay. Mr. Joseph Pursell, undergoing trial in 1805, was lucky that he was a poor man and the county had to pay for the jury's upkeep. During just one day of deliberation, the jury consumed five and one-half quarts of Madeira wine, two quarts of brandy, two quarts of beer, and one quart of cider. The records do not reveal what crime was charged, what verdict the jury came in with, or, indeed, if they were in any condition to come in with a verdict at all.

From all of the foregoing, it can be seen that the United States of America emerged with a jury system comparable to and in direct extension of the English jury. Variations there were, but it was determined at the very beginning that the jury was to be the American way of judicial determination. Although not always used, as will be seen, the twelve men in the jury box became the cornerstone of our judicial process.

4 The Jury in the American States Today

PEOPLE AND LEGISLATURES being what they are, it will not come as much of a surprise that in the fifty states of the Union, there are fifty variations of laws affecting the right to a jury trial. No two are exactly alike.

What is more of a surprise is that no two are completely different. Forty-four out of the fifty states proclaim the right to trial by jury to be held inviolate in their constitutions, in both civil and criminal cases. In Colorado and Wyoming, this right as set forth in the state constitutions, applies to criminal cases only; in Utah, to very serious criminal cases, calling for capital punishment. In North Carolina and Indiana, the right is held inviolate in civil cases.

One of the important areas of disagreement is the question of unanimity of verdict. Try to get eleven of your friends and yourself to agree on anything. These are people you know, quite likely with similar tastes and interests, yet they probably don't all agree. How can twelve strangers, deliberately chosen to emanate from varied walks of life, be expected to agree on matters of property, money, even life or death?

But they do. Surprisingly enough, it is an uncommon event when a jury must admit to a trial judge that it is hopelessly deadlocked, a "hung" jury.

It happens often enough, however, for some legislatures to have made it a little easier on the administrators of justice by providing for less than unanimous verdicts. Usually this is permitted in civil cases, that is, cases where no crime is involved and the issue involves only money or other rights not affecting life or liberty.

States that allow a verdict from three-quarters of the jury in civil cases are Alaska, Arizona, Arkansas, California, Hawaii, Idaho, Kentucky, Mississippi, Missouri (in courts of record), Nevada, Ohio, Oklahoma, Oregon, South Dakota, Texas, Utah, and Washington. Five-sixths is the number required in civil cases in Michigan, Nebraska, New Jersey, New York, Wisconsin, and Minnesota. (In Minnesota, however, the five-sixths rule only comes into play after the jury has deliberated for six hours, on the basis that if the jury is having that difficult a time agreeing, let's make it a little easier for them.) In Montana, the number is two-thirds, as it is in Missouri in courts not of record. New Mexico provides only that the legislature may set a less than unanimous vote.

As to less than unanimous verdicts in criminal cases, states that provide for such verdicts are Idaho (⅚ths vote), Montana (⅔rds vote in crimes less than felonies, which are major crimes), Oklahoma (¾ths vote for crimes less than felonies), Oregon (ten out of twelve, except in first degree murder cases, when the vote must be unanimous), and Texas (nine out of twelve in crimes less than felonies).

Oddly enough, the Supreme Court of the United States, in 1970, observed indirectly that the Federal requirement of unanimity was still unresolved with regard to any binding effect on state courts.

A word as to the terms "court of record" and "court not of record" would be in order here. In its loosest sense, a court of record is one in which more serious cases, both civil and criminal, are handled. Stenographic records of the proceedings are kept and are available if there is an appeal and judicial review of the proceedings. Conversely, courts not of record deal with lesser matters, and controversies or violations are dealt with on a much more informal basis. This may give some clue as to why strict adherence to the old English rule of twelve-man unanimous verdicts is cut down in courts not of record in so many states. The very work load of these lesser courts dictates time-saving expediencies.

Another watering-down of the old rights is the practice of providing for less than twelve-man juries. In over half of the states, the constitution provides (or the legislature has been empowered to so enact) for reduction in the number of jurors. This applies mainly in civil cases and there are slight variations from state to state, but the jury may be less than twelve in Alaska, Arizona, Colorado, Georgia, Iowa, Michigan, Missouri, Nebraska, New Jersey, New Mexico, North Dakota, Oklahoma, South Carolina, South Dakota, Utah, Washington, and Wyoming. Reduction in the number of jurors constituting a jury is prevalent in California, Colorado, Florida, Idaho, Illinois, Kentucky, Montana, Texas, Virginia, and West Virginia, with misdemeanor cases (lesser crimes) being included in some instances, as well as civil cases.

In Virginia, the Assembly may set different numbers of jurors for different offenses. Louisiana has an interesting rule regarding criminal cases. If punishment for the crime is not at hard labor, trial is by judge alone. In cases where there is a possibility that the punishment may be hard labor, a jury of five must reach a unanimous verdict. Where the sentence would be absolutely required to be hard labor, the jury would be twelve in number, with nine required to reach a verdict. Where the sentence would involve capital punishment, a unanimous verdict of a jury of twelve is required.

Following the trend, New York City, in April of 1971, reduced the number of jurors required in its Civil Court, a court of lesser jurisdiction dealing with civil matters, to six.

In 1970, the question of whether twelve-man juries were constitutionally required in state courts was raised, and the Supreme Court decided they were not.

Usually, the judge is the decider of the law and the jury is the trier of the facts. That is, the judge alone determines the applicability of statutes and other constituent parts of the law to the particular case before him, and the jury is bound by his statement to them of what the applicable law is. The jury must determine the facts within the framework of the law as outlined by the judge. In two states, the founders were so zealous with regard to the jury's powers, as distinguished from those of the judge, that the jury was made triers of both the law and the facts. This is so in Indiana and in criminal trials in Maryland.

In many states, money makes a difference in the right to a jury trial. Probably tied to the cynical Latin expression, *De minimus non curat lex*, (freely translated, "The Law doesn't worry about little things"), three states have granted the right to a jury in civil matters where the amount in controversy exceeds an arbitrary sum. In Alaska, the amount is $250, in Hawaii, it is $100, and in New Hampshire, $500. It is interesting to note that two of the jurisdictions mentioned are our newest states, perhaps representing the modern trend to limit the right to jury trials in civil cases.

In most of our states, there is a fee in civil cases for the right to demand a jury. In the Supreme Court of the State of New York, for instance, the cost of a six-man jury is $17.50, and for a twelve-man jury, $35, no matter which party in the case demands the jury.

Why would one party demand a six-man jury in a civil case and another a twelve-man jury? Most defendants feel that six persons on a jury will be a small enough group so that a "radical" verdict might emanate from it, especially in negligence cases. A verdict is the finding of the jury, their decision in the case, and a radical verdict would be a finding by the jury awarding an overly generous sum of money to the person suing. In automobile accident cases, in which an insurance company will have to pay any judgment against the defendant, small juries will sometimes go overboard on the amount of the verdict. Twelve-man juries, however, have enough diverse opinions represented so that any extreme opinion would be substantially diluted.

Not everyone wants a jury to decide his case. This may seem strange, in view of what you have read about the struggle by the People to retain the jury system for themselves and their countries, but it must be remembered that "the People" is not a homogeneous group, but is composed in part of persons and organizations that would not be the recipients of public sympathy in a public trial. For instance, most people tend to side with tenants over landlords, or with individuals over large corporations. Many persons have an instinctive mistrust of the driving abilities of taxi, bus, and truck operators in automobile accident cases. In addition, there might be a complicated set of facts in the case, many technicalities that would best be decided by one judge well versed in the intricacies of the law, rather than by a group of strangers who will decide basically on their human sympathies.

In civil cases, in most states, the right to trial by jury is waived if it is not demanded by a certain stage in the proceedings. Of course, if one of the parties does demand it, the fact that the other party would like to waive a jury makes no difference. The case will be tried before a jury.

Waiver of a jury in criminal cases is a more serious matter, although today all states permit waiver in some form or another. In 1930, the United States Supreme Court decided that a defendant in a Federal criminal case could waive a jury. This gave great impetus to the view that the right to a jury trial was a privilege to be exercised for the benefit of the accused and could be waived, as opposed to the view that a jury trial was the prescribed method of trial and could not be waived.

The Supreme Court felt some misgivings about waiver, however. It said, in another decision, that the effect of the waiver was so extreme, considering the place the jury system has in our traditions, that the judge and the prosecutor in Federal cases should be required to consent on the record to such waiver and should be required to explain fully such a step to the defendant.

The majority of states and the Federal courts now place qualifications on the right to waive a jury in criminal cases, but because of the case loads in the courts, and because non-jury trials take up only a fraction of the time jury trials do, the qualifications are, in most instances, disregarded in favor of waiver of jury. Many states have enacted statutory authority for waiver in criminal cases. The Supreme Court of the United States has ruled that such a state law which gives a defendant in a criminal case the right to waive trial by jury and be tried by a judge alone does not conflict with the Constitution of the United States of America.

As a further dilution of the right to trial by jury, it has been held by the highest courts that the right is not available to just any person who may suffer punishment or loss of property. In many cases where the cause of action or crime was not known under common law when we became a nation, or the right was not available to a party at that time, it has been held that it is not necessarily available now. In criminal cases, the right to trial by jury was somewhat restricted under the common law. In England jury trials were limited to "indictable offenses," those akin to our felonies, or more serious crimes. Other crimes were tried before magistrates.

America adopted this rule and enlarged upon it. However, it has never been fully tested whether the Constitution of the United States requires, under due process, a right to trial by jury in *all* criminal cases. This is because no state has as yet attempted to abolish jury trials for serious crimes.

The states have various degrees of availability of a jury trial. Some permit jury trials only in major cases and, of course, the number of jury trials in these states is small. In Connecticut in 1955, for example, there were only 66 criminal jury trials, or three jury trials per hundred thousand population, compared with the national average of approximately 35 per hundred thousand. In the same year, in Georgia, there were 144 criminal jury trials per hundred thousand population.

Minor crimes—disorderly conduct, prostitution, public drunkenness, certain traffic violations, minor forms of gambling—form a huge part of the work load of the criminal courts and the entire administration of justice would break down if lengthy jury trials were required in all these offenses. The fact that many states don't allow juries in this type of case can be chalked up to the practicalities of the situation.

The Supreme Court has recently broadened the base

of the right to trial by jury in criminal cases. Certain types of misdemeanors (lesser crimes) where punishment may involve one year's imprisonment, and in some cases, six months, are now subject to being tried before a jury. Since this is by far the most numerous type of case before the court, it has been the feeling that the court calendars would be swamped and the entire administration of justice might be endangered. Should justice, however, be curtailed by unproved "practical" considerations?

One sidelight of this problem, which, in effect, partially negates this recent decision, is the question of probation or sentencing to a reformatory. Though the case may be one where the maximum sentence may be minimal, a judge may direct probation for a long time, possibly three or four years or more, or may sentence a juvenile to a reformatory for an indeterminate time, amounting to several years.

Chief Justice Earl Warren of the Supreme Court, in 1969, stated that "the inescapable effect of this [development] will be to put a new weapon for chilling political expression in the unrestrained hands of trial judges."

Juveniles before the court also have difficulties in this regard. The purpose of treating them differently is to avoid labeling them as criminals if they are found guilty. This is a worthwhile aim, but in receiving such "preferred" treatment, many of the usual constitutional safeguards are not available to them. True, juries are available in serious juvenile matters in some jurisdictions, but this is far from universal. A 1971 decision of the Supreme Court stated that a juvenile court judge "may" have an advisory jury. The practice under this ruling will probably be to have the same informal procedure before the judge alone. The question that arises can best be stated: Is this sympathetic treatment or incarceration by another name?

Further indices of due process which juveniles may be entitled to, but of which they are sometimes deprived, are written notices of the charges against them, cross examination, privilege against self-incrimination, and the right to avail themselves of the presumption of innocence until proven guilty beyond a reasonable doubt. As the fight against such deprivation continues, should not the fight against the deprivation of trial by jury, as a universal rule in serious matters affecting juveniles, be pressed?

Some areas still regard "trial by a jury of one's peers" as just that. In Denver, recently, a juvenile court judge dismissed the entire panel inasmuch as it had been proven to his satisfaction that there had been a systematic exclusion of people twenty-one to thirty years old from the panel.

The concept that the jury must be from the area where the crime was committed was an old and firmly established one. The reasons for this are obvious: the jurors should represent the conscience of that particular community. What would be held abhorrent in one area could be regarded as quite normal in another area. To this day, the same rule usually applies in the various courts of the land.

However, it sometimes becomes necessary to change the place of trial, or, as it is called, the venue. In today's modern society, with its deluge of news and opinion flowing from the press, radio, and television, there is rarely such a thing as an uninformed juror, especially in spectacular crimes that have been played up by the news media and have inflamed the emotions and sensibilities in the community where the crime occurred.

Recently in Chicago, eight nurses were murdered at one time in a most garish manner. With the news media screaming for blood and quick justice and condemning the accused killer even before his capture, there would be little likelihood that the court system in Chicago would be able to muster sufficient unprejudiced jurors. The nature of the crime was heinous, but the point that had to be decided was whether the particular accused individual did it. Wisely, a change of venue was ordered and the trial was held in a different part of the state.

However, a change of venue, considering the widespread coverage of the media, is not always a solution. Since the beginning of our nation, there has always been a conflict between the First Amendment, dealing with freedom of the press, and the Sixth Amendment, dealing with fair trials before an impartial jury. The topic has come to a head in recent years.

In July of 1788, three years before the Bill of Rights, a Pennsylvania court punished a litigant for contempt because of public statements made to all and sundry, which would have affected the possibility of empaneling an impartial jury.

Feeling its power, the position of the press was epitomized in 1830 by James Gordon Bennett when he stated, "The press is the living jury of the nation."

The subject of the press and a fair trial mostly deals with the impact of the jurors. Does informing (and at times inflaming) the citizenry constitute a danger to a fair trial, or only to ignorance? Must the population take sides even before a trial? After all, legal trials are not elections. If unrestricted pre-trial publicity were allowed to make people choose sides before the presentation of evidence, would this not be akin to the doctrine of the Nazis? Under their general penal law, anyone could be punished "who deserves punishment" under "the sound feeling of the nation."

For instance, in a 1961 Louisiana case, a confession was televised over a local station, and the court refused to oust three jurors who had seen the telecast. Despite the fact that the confession was never introduced into evidence for perfectly good legal reasons, the defendant was found guilty, such finding being reversed on appeal. In this instance, the telecast was his trial.

In January of 1967, a judge in Berkeley, California, held two defendants who had been campus sit-ins in contempt for holding a press conference in violation of a court order. As the judge stated, "The order was made to assure them of a fair trial."

In the last few years, at least six verdicts were reversed because of unfair pre-trial publicity, and this is only the tip of the iceberg.

It is claimed by those who advocate untrammeled pre-trial publicity that between 1955 and 1965 only 3 per cent of newspaper space was devoted to crime news. Can there be any doubt, however, that lurid crime news sells newspapers?

In England, the contempt power is widely used against newspapers. Here, it is sparingly used, if ever. Unbounded pre-trial publicity—is it the watchdog of our democratic system or the cancer within the right to an impartial jury?

In addition, in many states, change of venue is allowed where the judge in the district is a near relative of either the prosecutor or defendant, has knowledge of the facts which would make it possible for him to be a witness, or if there are any set of facts showing that the defendant would not be likely to receive a fair trial in that particular district.

This is the general picture of the right to a jury trial in the United States of America today. It is a flourishing system with broad application, held sacred and indefeasible in most instances. Although hedged here and there with certain restrictions, it has retained its place as one of the best of the people's safeguards.

5 Turning Citizens into Jurors

To THIS POINT, we have been dealing somewhat in an abstraction, the right to a jury trial. We have generally observed the mechanics of the jury system among the ancients. Now let us explore the modern-day mechanism for turning citizens into jurors.

Across America, in almost all states, there is a fairly standard method of accomplishing this. Usually, there is a body of men appointed for each area or each court, known as a jury commission. It is their job to provide lists of prospective jurors in sufficient quantities as will meet the respective needs of each court. There are various means of assembling the names, whether it be from local assessment rolls, voting records, other tax rolls or some other source.

As a rule, there is a conscious effort on the part of the commissioners to seek a cross section of the population on the jury panel. Generally, the names chosen must meet certain basic requirements, such as the ability to read and write English, the absence of a serious criminal record, being between certain ages, and in good health. Certain citizens who are important to the carrying out of the day-to-day functions of the community, such as doctors, druggists, and firemen, may be specifically exempted.

Of course there must be no systematic exclusion of a group because of race, creed, politics, or occupation. In many states, there have been such attempted exclusions, and there have been numerous court battles as a result.

In a recent series of cases, the problem has arisen as to whether a person may be excluded from a jury solely on the grounds that he does not subscribe to the death penalty. Until now, this has been a standard ground of challenge for cause. The decisions have now seemed to indicate that there can be no such outright challenge unless the prospective juror is not only against the death penalty, but would be found not to be able to judge impartially if death might be a verdict.

In a lighter mood, systematic exclusion was recently requested. A female defendant requested an all-girl jury, but this was denied. It was held that a jury of one's peers only means a representative selection of members of the community, not exact sex, age, and so on.

In some states, as unfair as it may seem, there is still exclusion of women as jurors. In other states, they are called only if they volunteer for such service. This follows the old common law under which women were not allowed to serve.

There are differences from state to state, but let us examine the process of selecting jurors in one state, which will serve to illustrate the details of all.

New York is, like most states, made up of disparate types of community living. There are the vast stretches of farmland, dotted with small communities; the labyrinths of the metropolis; the medium-sized typical American city and town. Each of these areas naturally requires a different system of obtaining jurors, considering the quantity and quality of the potential panelists available.

To cope with this problem, New York state law established three separate divisions under its Judiciary Law. The first is that of small counties, under 100,000 population, where the county elects to come under these special regulations. At the other extreme, we have counties within cities having a population of one million or more. In between, there is the county with the moderate population, not by any means to be considered sparsely populated, but not a huge metropolis either.

In the small counties, the supervisor, town clerk, and tax assessors of each town meet once a year and prepare a list of persons to serve as trial jurors. The trial jury lists are the sources of names for the grand jury lists, in the event that a grand jury is required to decide if there is enough evidence to require a man to stand trial.

Town assessment rolls are the primary sources of names for trial jury lists, but other directories may be used as well, such as the latest census enumeration, the telephone directory, the voters' registry, or other general sources of names.

Not everyone on such a list would qualify as a trial juror in New York state. A prospective juror must be a citizen of the United States of America and a resident of the county, between twenty-one and seventy-two years of age, be of sound mind and not infirm, "be of good character, of approved integrity, of sound judgment," and able to read and write English. Such a person must not have been convicted of a felony or a misdemeanor involving moral turpitude, that is, something morally bad. Up until September of 1967, such a person must have been the owner or the spouse of the owner of land or personal property worth at least two hundred and fifty dollars.

It is most puzzling how one can discern from a telephone directory or a town assessment roll that a human being is of approved integrity and has sound judgment. A good deal of the selection, of necessity, must be of the "pig-in-a-poke" variety. And yet, the system, by and large, works.

As distinguished from exemptions, where the exemption usually must be claimed before the person is discharged from jury duty, certain categories of people are completely disqualified. Among such persons are elected officials of the Federal government all the way down to village officers, certain state officials, congressmen and other legislators, judges, sheriffs, and clerks of courts.

With regard to exemptions, it must be remembered that these are people who are entitled to sit as jurors. Only by their affirmative acts of negation are they relieved of such duty. A sampling of those who can be exempted from jury service are doctors, dentists, pharmacists, clergymen, lawyers, service men, firemen, policemen, ships' officers, certain newspaper officials, women, and embalmers.

When the lists of prospective jurors are prepared in these small communities, the name is kept on the list for one year and such person may be called during that time. When it is time for the citizen to serve, the sheriff notifies him that he has been selected for that particular term.

Approximately once a month, there is a new term for each court. The law provides the means of drawing the names of prospective jurors for that term out of a box, the names being the ones prepared in the towns by the commissioners. The section of the New York law that provides for this goes into fine details, such as who must be present at the drawing and even states, rather primly, that "The clerk must shake the box containing the ballots, so as thoroughly to mix them." Thoughtfully, the law adds that if any name drawn is that of a person who is dead or insane, that person may not be used and the ballot with his name on it is to be destroyed.

A person who desires to obtain such a list may do so by paying a small fee. Of course, this is usually only done in important cases in which the lawyer for either party wants to investigate the prospective jurors before meeting them in court, so as to know their prejudices and backgrounds, whom to accept, and whom to reject for a jury.

The trial judge has the right to excuse a juror for good cause shown, or to postpone his term of service, since jury duty was not meant to produce an undue hardship on a citizen. The prospective juror may be excused if his or the public's interest may be materially injured, if he is a party in an action at that time, if his own health is involved or there is death or sickness in his immediate family. However, one of the sad failings of a few of our citizens is the attempt to "duck" jury service just because it would be a minor inconvenience. Many are the strange and wonderful tales of fancied ailments and other problems that judges hear over the years from disgruntled prospective jurors.

The usual reason for seeking excusal from jury duty is that the average person, a working or business man, will suffer in one way or another if he has to stay away from work. In many cases, this is true. However, there is a section in the law that states that an employer cannot discharge an employee for jury duty, though he need not pay him for the time lost. Certain large companies, in the proper spirit, not only have no objections to their employees sitting on jury duty, but even make up the loss in wages.

Another reason for seeking to avoid jury duty is the fear of the unknown, possibly of the difficult examination they think the lawyers will put them through. This fear is largely a figment of the imagination, as most lawyers are much more afraid of the jurors or, at least, of offending them, than the jurors are afraid of the lawyers.

Special provisions are made for grand jurors. Grand juries are those jury panels in criminal cases to which the prosecutor applies for an indictment, that is, an accusation against some individual considered guilty of a serious crime. Only the prosecutor's side is heard, usually, and unanimity is not required. The grand jury usually consists of not less than sixteen nor more than twenty-three people, a quorum of sixteen being necessary to conduct business. To vote an indictment, twelve must concur. Since the grand jury is usually twenty-three, this would constitute a bare majority. The indictment is merely an accusation,

and cannot be used as evidence at a trial. It merely requires the defendant to stand public trial. Usually, if the
grand jury does not find an indictment, the person has a
good chance of not being prosecuted, although this is not
always true. A prosecutor who is dissatisfied with one
jury's finding of no indictment, may take the same case to
another grand jury.

Much unrest has arisen throughout the nation recently
with regard to the operations of the grand jury, and even
to the institution itself.

The claim is made that under the present procedure of
holding grand jury deliberations, as outlined above, the
grand jury becomes just a rubber stamp of the prosecutor.
In cases of potential publicity, some unscrupulous prosecutors seek only the indictment, and the actual results of
the trial get lost in fresher news at a later time.

For instance, during the 1951 Senate hearings on crime,
more than forty indictments were handed down for contempt of Congress because the witnesses pleaded their
constitutional privileges against self-incrimination. There
was not even one conviction, but the final result made
no headlines.

Another issue raised is whether the grand jury has been
used to harass dissident groups and punish unfriendly
witnesses who appear before it.

A suggested replacement for the grand jury is a judge
who will decide if there is enough proof to even bring the
case to trial. In some states, such as Michigan, the judge
gets run-of-the-mill cases for indictments, and a grand
jury gets general investigations. At least eighteen states

have abolished the grand jury entirely and three states partially. It has been calculated that one judge can handle the job that could be handled by three panels.

However, is the issue a problem of stronger-willed grand jurors or more responsible prosecutors? Would a jaded judge represent the conscience of the community?

Grand jurors do often refuse to indict. They even often rebel at improper tactics of the prosecutor, such as in a California case in late 1971 when three grand jurors walked out of the deliberations because of the alleged misconduct of the prosecutor.

In addition, a judge in New York in 1969 set aside an indictment upon reading the grand jury minutes, because of the improper actions of the prosecutor. If the prosecutor had the right to have a person indicted without such a hearing, on his own motion, where would the rein on his powers have been in this case?

With respect to the qualifications of the grand juror, he may be challenged for various reasons, among them the fact that he is a minor, an alien, insane, a prosecutor on a charge against the defendant, a witness for either party, there is evidence that he cannot act with impartiality, or the court feels he is prejudiced.

Of late, there have been challenges as to how grand jurors are selected. A survey used in an attack on the system in Bronx County, New York City, was made by the Center for Urban Education. This group found that, in 1967, the grand jury in the Bronx was composed of people of whom 90 per cent were white, 66 per cent earned more than $10,000 per year, only 3.5 per cent earned less than

$5,000 per year, 8 per cent were Negroes and 1.1 per cent were Puerto Ricans. The make-up of the county at the same time indicated that almost half of the residents earned less than $5,000 per year and the "non-white" residents constituted 38 per cent of the population. Is this a true cross section of the community?

A case that reached the United States Supreme Court challenged the system in New York County. The roster of prospective grand jurors included 1.65 per cent Negroes and .03 per cent Puerto Ricans, while at the same time, the residents of the county included 24 per cent Negroes and 9 per cent Puerto Ricans. The court, however, found that there was no "intentional and systematic discrimination" against these groups.

Volunteers for grand jury duty are being attacked, since many of them are found to be friends or relatives of correction officers and others in the legal apparatus, and have a vested interest in hard and fast "law and order."

Throughout the land, the current attempt to eliminate discrimination against minorities and the poor, modeled after recent Federal legislation, requires the use of a single source of potential grand jurors, voter registration lists. In many states, this change in procedure has taken effect already. In addition, the subjective tests which were often used to eliminate certain types—such tests as "intelligence," "of sound mind," "well-informed," and "of good character"—are being replaced with the objective test of the ability to read, write, speak, and understand English.

The grand jury can inquire into corrupt misconduct in

office of public officers of every description, and also into the condition and management of the public prisons within the county. Assuming that the grand jury does not feel there are sufficient grounds to indict a public official, but feels that there is a bad situation which the public should know about, it makes an open presentment so that the citizenry will know of its findings.

The same qualifications, disqualifications, and exemptions apply to trial jurors, adding, however, as possible exemptions, teachers, professors, and the like. If one man, through some quirk of fate, has his name chosen for both the trial juror and grand juror lists, the grand jury takes precedence.

The next political subdivision that the law encompasses is the metropolis, the county within cities having a population of one million or more. In these counties, the county clerk is charged with responsibility for selecting, drawing, summoning, and empanelling all trial jurors within his county. In accordance with the rules laid down above for smaller counties, he rules on the qualifications, disqualifications, and exemptions of such prospective jurors. With several other county officials he selects the future grand jurors.

The qualifications of prospective jurors in the big cities are substantially the same as for the small counties discussed earlier. The county clerk is given latitude to determine qualifications, and a court will not usually overrule him. In one case, a person who had been blind since birth sought to become a juror, but the county clerk felt that he was disqualified because he was not in possession of all of his natural faculties. The court upheld the county clerk.

Occasionally there are times when the clerk is overruled. In one instance, a person with violent religious prejudices, completely contrary to the fundamentals of religious tolerance and freedom, was sought to be excluded on the grounds that the law required the juror to be "intelligent" and that by holding such beliefs, he was not "intelligent." The court thought otherwise and reversed the decision of the county clerk.

In many places automation has taken over the arduous task of selecting and summoning the jurors. In New York City in May of 1960, 1,300 jurors were called for service in the Supreme, City, Municipal, and General Sessions Courts. In twenty-five minutes, automatic IBM machines mixed the punch cards, selected the jurors, typed out the lists of jurors, and typed and mailed the summonses.

Ordinarily, the juror will receive at least ten days notice of being called for jury duty. Any juror wanting to be excused must present the summons served upon him personally in court, and must give written proof of absence from the city at the time of service or of physical disability by way of a physician's certificate.

When a person has been called for jury duty, a representative of the county clerk interviews him at the clerk's office, a questionnaire is filled out, and the person's name may be forwarded to the police department to see if the person has a criminal record. This last procedure is definitely followed with the grand juror. In fact, the prospective grand juror's fingerprints are taken, thus helping to check through the proper authorities as to whether such a person has a criminal record or not. Not every crime that may be listed on the record of a prospective grand juror is reason for disqualification; only if the crime is a felony (a serious crime) or a misdemeanor involving moral turpitude.

Disqualification may occur as a result of intelligence tests given by the clerk. Suppose a man makes a living with his hands and knows little of reading or writing English, and thereby fails the test. Admittedly, this manual laborer is deprived of the general right to participate in his government as a juror. Admittedly, the jury, which is supposed to be a true cross section of the community, loses a disproportionately high amount of manual laborers and is therefore not truly representative. Yet, the court has said that in weighing equities, the condition must continue because in most cases it is far more important that the juror understand what is going on and be able to read any exhibits placed in evidence—in short, that he must read and write English—than that true cross-representation must be preserved for its own sake.

Unlike the smaller counties, the county clerk of the heavily populated county notifies the jurors of prospective service either by mail, personally, or by leaving the notice at the juror's residence with a person "of suitable age."

Considering the variety of courts in the larger cities, and the number of them, the law arranges for cross-shifting of jurors between courts, wherever there is a need for jurors within that county.

The third area is the one consisting of counties too large

for the under-one-hundred-thousand population counties and outside of the million-plus cities. This subdivision uses a county jury board system to arrange for the procurement of jurors, with a commissioner to do the actual work. Using the same sources of names as the other two sub-divisions, the commissioner may either mail questionnaires to the prospective jurors or summon them to his office to fill them out. The qualifications and disqualifications are substantially the same in this type of county as the others, except that the age limit for a juror may be seventy-two years instead of seventy.

The trial jurors are required to sit as potential jury panel members from five days to two weeks, but the practice is to have them sit for the full two weeks. Grand jurors sit for the term of the court for which a grand jury is drawn or, if they sit for less than five days, they may be called for another term. Once having served, both trial and grand jurors may not be called again for two years.

In New York City and many other communities the juror receives twelve dollars per day for his time, plus carfare.

How does a panel member actually get on a jury? He is sitting in the jury assembly room with desks, pens, telephones, and paper all at hand so that he may continue his regular work in what manner he can. He is even permitted to consult briefly with office associates and employees. While in the jury assembly room his name has been placed on a card and inserted in a special box, usually a rotating drum, which has a small door. When it is time to empanel a jury the ballots are drawn from the drum, one by one, until the full panel is chosen. This, of course, is not the final jury. Much has to happen before the actual jury is selected for a particular trial.

There have been some innovations with regard to procedure, especially in the big cities. With so many cases being marked ready each day in each court, there are times when one court has too many jurors and another court has exhausted its panel. In addition, there is tremendous duplication of effort for getting jurors to particular courts. As a result there has arisen a Central Jury System in various communities whereby a central agency obtains the jurors for all the courts and distributes them according to need.

The procedures discussed here apply to state courts only. A separate procedure exists for Federal courts, that is, United States courts which try cases involving Federal laws or cases between citizens of different states.

As there are fifty states, so there are fifty means of turning citizens into jurors, but underneath, they are all akin. There is the gathering of names from general sources, the qualifications, disqualifications and exemptions, the random calling of jurors for stated terms, and the narrowing down of the field through interrogation. But with the preliminaries out of the way, the jury is set to embark on the same road of decision first trod by the ancients.

6 The Federal System

THE BASIS FOR JURIES in the Federal courts rests on Article III, Section 2, of the Constitution of the United States (jury trials in criminal cases), and Constitutional amendments Five (indictment by grand jury), Six (speedy trial by jury in the state and district where the crime was committed), and Seven (the jury in civil cases).

Prior to 1948, the applicable Federal law provided that jurors summoned to serve in the Federal courts had to have the same qualifications and be entitled to the same exemptions as jurors in the state in which the district court was located. This was an old rule, tracing its way back to the Judiciary Act of 1789, and under it, a uniform Federal system of jury selection was impossible, since the Federal juries were subject to all the infirmities and prejudices of each state. Certain state laws were weighted against various elements of the population—Negroes, wage earners, women. Some states went so far as to exempt accountants, chiropodists, and linotype operators.

In 1948, a Federal law was passed providing for uniform qualifications, exemptions, and excuses from service of jurors for Federal courts. The law retained, however, the restriction that if a juror was incompetent to serve by virtue of the law in the state where the court sat, he could not be a Federal juror. This was, in effect, only a partial improvement and in 1957, the selection of persons to serve as jurors in Federal courts was then established solely by Act of Congress.

In 1968, Congress enacted the Federal Jury Selection and Service Act, truly the first attempt to deal with grand jury and petit jury selection in a systematic manner. Based upon the growing feeling that the business of deciding who was to be on a jury panel was not simply an administrative task that should be left to a clerk, and the further desire to open up jury service to many who have not had a previous opportunity, the Act was designed to obtain a true cross section of the community on the jury.

In the past, clerks had made snap judgments (possibly masking bias) as to the "common sense" or "intelligence" of a prospective juror. In addition, a disproportionately large number of those from the rural areas or small towns were never called, since they were so far from the courthouse.

Now, prospective jurors are, by and large, chosen from voter lists by random selection. Only objective criteria may be used, such as age, citizenship, literacy, health, and absence of a criminal record.

The Act also no longer automatically exempts women, although they may be excused if they have children under ten years of age. Furthermore, the old lists are discarded every four years, and new ones are drawn. This results in a situation wherein a prospective juror will not be called on eight to ten occasions, but will probably be called only once in a lifetime.

This has resulted in a sharp increase in the number of qualified jurors.

Today, a prospective Federal grand or petit juror must have the following qualifications:

1. A citizen of the United States of America
2. Over twenty-one years of age
3. A resident of the judicial district for at least one year
4. Not convicted of a crime punishable by more than one year in jail
5. Able to read, write, speak, and understand English
6. Not mentally or physically infirm

Federal jurors may be exempted from service if they are members of the armed forces in active service, a policeman, fireman, or a public official. The law spells out these specific exemptions, but the district judge is also empowered to excuse an individual if such service would cause undue hardship, extreme inconvenience, or serious obstruction or delay in the fair and impartial administration of justice.

Federal judges are also empowered to exclude entire groups if he finds that the service of the people in such a class would cause such hardship, inconvenience, or obstruction. Such types are usually doctors, lawyers, and clergymen. It is deemed to be for the betterment of the community if these people are kept at their professional duties. The aged are sometimes excluded also.

Judges are cautious about exempting individuals, but

are quite liberal in granting postponements of service so as to more conveniently suit the schedule of the prospective juror.

Of course, it would be best if the court clerks would check in advance as to the best time for jurors to serve, but, practically, this is difficult to do, and most clerks make no such attempt. In a few jurisdictions, the jurors, when qualifying, note their months of preference and are called at that time.

The two people in charge of procuring names and selecting Federal jurors are the clerk of the district court and a jury commissioner. These two, who by law must be members of opposite political parties, constitute the Federal Jury Commission for the district.

Before the new law went into effect, there were instances of discrimination in selection of prospective Federal jurors. In 1957, jury commissioners in a district in California had deliberately excluded women from the panels, despite the fact that California state law did not so exclude them. In a test case, the Supreme Court of the United States struck down the exclusion of women from Federal juries. Today, the law says specifically that women are eligible to serve.

There is economic discrimination as well. The clerk and the jury commissioner in a particular district, again in California, were systematically excluding daily wage earners. Their excuse was that such service would be a hardship on these wage earners and that the judge would in all probability excuse them anyway. In declaring unlawful this form of discrimination, the Supreme Court said:

The American tradition of trial by jury . . . necessarily contemplates an impartial jury drawn from a cross section of the community. This does not mean, of course, that every jury must contain representatives of all the economic, social, religious, racial, political and geographical groups of the community . . . it does mean that prospective jurors shall be selected by court officials without systematic and intentional exclusion of any of these groups.

Possibly the most explosive and dangerous form of discrimination is with regard to race. Although there has been no overt evidence of this in the Federal courts, there have been instances of it in the state courts, which affects the Federal court jury system by indirect means.

In a 1950 Texas case, the jury commissioners chose only from among people they knew and believed to be eligible. Because they allegedly knew of no eligible Negroes, they chose no Negroes. This was held by the court to be discrimination. These men, charged with the task of finding responsible jurors who represented a cross section of the community, were obliged to familiarize themselves with the qualifications of the eligible jurors in their district—all the eligible jurors—Negro as well as white.

In Georgia, in 1953, the names of white jurors were put on white cards used for drawing, and the names of Negroes were put on yellow cards. As a result very few Negroes were ever called for jury duty. Once again the highest court in the land felt that this was a clear-cut case of discrimination.

There is a problem with volunteers for Federal jury duty. Nothing in the law prohibits the use of such volunteers, and they may be citizens motivated by the purest of patriotic zeal. Not all motives for volunteering are so praiseworthy, however. It may be recalled that the ancient Greek *dikasts,* or jurors, were preponderantly comprised of the poor, seeking avidly for the pittance the *dikasts* were paid. There has grown up in many metropolitan areas a class of professional jurors who make a partial living from the relatively small jury fee. There also have been instances of mobsters attempting to place undesirable and controlling elements on jury panels, in order to try to rig criminal prosecutions. Most district clerks do not accept volunteers. A few districts do, but tend to screen these people with a great deal of care.

Usually, Federal jurors serve for two weeks, although in many districts the length of service runs to three weeks or more.

When the lists are complete, the process of selecting those who will be jurors begins. In about two-thirds of the Federal districts questionnaires are sent out, to eliminate those who do not have the requisite qualifications or who would be granted blanket exemption by the court. Either the clerk, commissioner, or judge, or a combination of them, makes the actual decision as to disqualification. Usually, no other investigation is made for the purpose of initial disqualification.

A more expensive method now in use in some districts is the personal interview by the clerk. (The prospective juror has to pay his own transportation.) Sometimes there is a mingling of the two means of initially selecting Federal jurors. In the District of Columbia, for example, personal interviews are used where there remains doubt in the proper official's mind, based on the completed questionnaire, as to the fitness of the juror with regard to intelligence, physical fitness to serve, and the like.

Once the names are approved, they go into the stream that constantly replenishes the "box" containing the names of jurors from which panels (or venires, as they are called) are drawn for a particular term of the court. The box must contain a minimum of three hundred names, but in many districts it runs into the thousands.

Most districts draw separate grand and petit (trial) jury venires. Almost all districts have several irreproachable officials on hand for the drawing, to insure impartiality, and one district has gone so far as to have a small child who cannot read or write draw the names.

Once the venire is selected, the jurors may be summoned by personal service, registered mail, or, as is now most commonly used, certified mail. Most districts permit jurors to mail in excuses before their term of service. The judge then passes on the excuses and the juror is advised of his decision. In a few districts, the clerk is allowed to excuse jurors. Petit jurors are not allowed to serve more than once a year.

The Federal jury system has been legally divorced from the constrictions of state laws and prejudices, and has become a comprehensive system of its own, with its own qualifications, disqualifications, and exemptions. The result is an independent body, highly intelligent for the most part, and a true and representative cross section of the community.

The Federal courts are now becoming more crowded with civil rights cases, many of them transfers from the state courts. Up until recently, there was only a trickle of such cases, starting with *habeas corpus* proceedings for dubious incarceration following the Civil War. The first reared its head in 1867, but all such cases were subject to the "exhaustion of states' remedies" doctrine. This meant that appeals would have to be pursued up through the highest court of the individual state before the Federal courts would assume jurisdiction.

Now, more use is being made of the Federal constitutional issue of denial of a fair trial to bring the matter directly before the Federal courts. Recent bases on which such jurisdiction was founded are claims of mob domination, systematic exclusion of minorities from the juries, and other examples of denial of due process.

There has even been espoused a right to remove a civil rights case to a Federal court from a state court before trial, especially when the right allegedly violated is a specific statutory right of racial equality.

It is for this very reason of an increased workload that the streamlining of the Federal jury procedure becomes most timely and vital.

7 Selecting the Jury

MELVIN BELLI, the famous west coast trial attorney, in the preface to his book *Modern Trials,* tells of selecting a juror in Las Vegas, Nevada. Upon asking a prospective juror his occupation, the man replied, "Gambler." Mr. Belli thought for a moment and responded, "I am a gambler, too, every time I go before a jury."

The truth of that rueful rejoinder rests on two bases. The first is the fact that of the two parties who are contending in the courtroom, unless the case is settled during trial or the jury cannot agree on the verdict, one of the two parties is going to walk out winning, the other losing. This, in theory, depends upon the strength of the case or defense, the prowess of the respective attorneys and the pre-trial investigation.

The other base of the gamble is the jury, that relatively unknown quantity, the ultimate weighers of the facts.

We have traced the jurors from their homes, through the questionnaires and investigations, to the moment when they actually report for jury duty. The venire is formed, the panel is assembled in the jury waiting room, waiting for their respective names to be called for actual use in a trial.

Somewhere in the same building, a judge has directed all lawyers involved in a particular case to pick a jury. The word is passed along to the court officials in charge of the jurors that a panel is needed.

Methods vary in the several states, but as a fairly representative system, let us assume that thirty names of prospective jurors are picked out of a revolving drum to form the panel for a particular trial, out of which twelve will be selected to be the actual jurors.

Twelve cards are picked out at random from the total number of cards representing the panel. These cards usually contain the name, address, and perhaps the occupation of the prospective juror. They are placed on a board divided into sections corresponding to the seats in the jury box, the enclosure where the jury sits while the trial is proceeding. The usual arrangement is two parallel rows of six seats, one row behind the other.

Now commences the *voir dire*. The term figuratively means "to speak the truth." It is actually a preliminary examination of the prospective juror to determine his qualifications, any reason for disqualification, or any bias he may have that would render him unfit for this particular jury.

Possibly the most important reason for the *voir dire* is to size up the prospective juror. Here is the opportunity for the lawyers to question this stranger, obtaining as much from the way he answers as from the answers themselves.

A bellicose juror, a friendly and open one, even one who counters a question with an evasion or a question of his own, reveals his personality and nature. This is the litigant's only day in court, the only time he will have to press his case or defend against it, and some insight must be gained into the stranger who will decide it if allowed to remain on the jury.

In many states, the lawyers handling the case do all of the questioning of the prospective juror. The judge, if present, may ask some questions. Unfortunately, this sometimes takes an inordinate amount of time, as over-zealous lawyers press home points many times covered. In other jurisdictions, the judge conducts most of the inquiry himself, thus substantially cutting down on the time for picking the jury. He permits the lawyers to ask supplementary questions or he inquires into such matters as the attorneys desire.

In no jurisdiction may the attorney be shut out completely from having questions he deems vital asked of the jurors. However, the course and extent of the *voir dire* is within the discretion of the trial judge.

In the Federal courts, the judge usually does most of the questioning, and counsel for both sides ask supplementary questions. However, the trial judge in the Federal system quite often permits the lawyers to do all of the interrogation. In almost all of the Federal districts, the jurors are subjected to the *voir dire* in the courtroom before the judge.

Questions have arisen in recent years as to the worth of the *voir dire* by the attorney, and the abuse of the privilege that has crept into the system. In 1969, the New Jersey Supreme Court, commenting on this, stated that many lawyers are using the questioning period to obtain a favorable, not an impartial, jury. The court recommended that the trial judge do most of the interrogation, with the attorneys permitted to supplement questions. The same experiment was tried in criminal cases in New York for a short while in 1971, but was dropped.

However, there is a serious question as to the value of this change of procedure. Hundreds of years ago, everyone in a small town where a trial was held knew each other. Now, we are all strangers to each other, and time must be taken to uncover hidden feelings. The judge may be superficial in his questioning, anxious to proceed to the next case, and the next. In our adversary type of practice, however, a person's attorney, concerned with his client's interests, may uncover prejudice or bias where a judge may gloss over it.

The usual order of questioning of the jurors by the lawyers starts with the attorneys for the plaintiff (in a civil case) or for the prosecutor (in a criminal case) asking questions. When he is finished, the defendant's attorney may ask questions.

The lawyers for each side have, primarily, three remedies for removing objectionable jurors. All three are known as challenges. The first is a challenge to the array; the second, challenge for cause; lastly, there is the peremptory challenge.

The challenge to the array is a challenge to the panel from which the jury is being drawn. It is based on the claim that the proper standards, constitutional and otherwise, have not been applied to obtaining jurors in that particular jurisdiction. This is the one challenge that seeks to sweep aside the entire panel. The other two challenges are as to individuals.

The challenge for cause means just that; there are circumstances involving this particular prospective juror that make him unfit to sit on this case. Many of these reasons for disqualification are codified by statute. There are various grounds for a challenge for cause. The prospective juror may be related to one of the parties, interested witnesses, or the attorneys. He may stand to benefit directly or indirectly by a decision for one side or the other. He may have a fixed opinion as to a certain situation, and nothing is going to change his mind. Perhaps he is not willing to listen to the judge as to the law, in effect, substituting his own judgment of what the law should be in place of the judge's instructions as to what the law is. In a case involving possible punishment, he may not believe in such punishment (especially where the punishment may be the death penalty).

On one occasion involving a taxicab driver in a civil suit, a prospective juror with a perfectly cheerful expression on his face volunteered the statement, "Actually, I hate cab drivers." Perhaps a little less cheerfully, and with the consent of the other lawyer, the attorney for the cab driver excused the gentleman. This was obvious bias and prejudice.

Most of the foregoing grounds are not susceptible to black and white determinations. The answer to a given question may indicate, in the mind of one of the attorneys, that a prospective juror has a fixed opinion on the subject of the lawsuit, that he is biased, that he may very well stand to gain as a result of the lawsuit. Here the judge must rule. If he overrules the challenge for cause, and an objection is made, there is the possibility of an appeal to a higher court after a verdict has been reached.

While being questioned, the potential juror is often unsworn and no record is made of the questions put to him and his replies. However, this does not mean that such juror may lie with impunity. The attorneys are entitled to truthful answers to their questions. It is the duty of the juror to disclose facts which may cause him to be biased. Although the legislature may limit the number of peremptory challenges, it cannot limit the number of challenges for cause, as this would be a denial of due process of law.

A challenge for cause may be waived by either side. There are not only voluntary waivers, there are involuntary waivers as well. A juror must be challenged for cause before he takes his oath at the start of a trial. Failure to challenge constitutes a waiver.

The last of the three challenges is the peremptory challenge. This is the "hunch" challenge. After many years of trial work, an attorney develops a sense as to the type of juror who would be best to sit on his client's case. There need be no legal reason whatsoever for the challenge. The judge cannot pass upon the challenge. Unlike the challenge for cause, where the number of such challenges is unrestricted, every state severely limits the number of peremptory challenges allowed each party. If it did not, such challenges could be made to every juror, and a lawyer whose party was not particularly eager to go to trial could indefinitely delay matters. In New York state courts, an attorney is allowed six peremptory challenges, as to a jury of twelve, and three challenges for a jury of six.

Over the years, certain conclusions have been reached by members of the Bar as guidelines in jury selection. Rightly or wrongly, these opinions play a large part in a lawyer's examination of a prospective jury.

Suitability and desirability are looked for. For instance, if ledgers and books of account are to play a vital part in the case, the question arises, is there anyone on the jury who understands bookkeeping? In involved cases, where a number of inextricably interwoven issues must be resolved, an intelligent jury will be sought, younger rather than older people, men rather than women.

In a civil case, where the plaintiff is a child, the attorney for the infant would want more women than men (they being supposedly more sympathetic to children), older rather than younger women, older rather than younger men, especially those who have children or grandchildren of their own. Where women are parties in the case, most lawyers are loathe to retain women jurors, since they are thought to be harder on their own sex. Of couse, if the party is a young, attractive man, the more women jurors the better.

If the plaintiff in a civil case is an older person, older rather than younger jurors are desired, since they can place themselves in the shoes of the older party, and can appreciate what pain and suffering mean at that stage of life.

There is a difference between new versus repeater jurors, those who have sat on juries on many occasions. Those who have never served before are felt to be a little more prone to grant the defendant in a criminal case the benefit of a reasonable doubt, or return a higher monetary verdict in a civil case.

Racial considerations constitute a touchy subject, but must be recognized as quite important to jury selection. It is assumed that if one of the parties is of a particular ethnic background, a juror with a like background will tend to side with him.

As to tendencies to favor one side more than the other, it is recognized that because of their leanings toward the underdog and the underprivileged, Irish, Italians, Jews, French, Negroes, people of Spanish-speaking ancestry and those of Balkan heritage will usually sympathize with the plaintiff in a civil suit and with the defendant in criminal matters. It is also believed that because of their uprightness and belief in a stern code of ethics, Englishmen, Scandinavians and Germans will vote in a directly contrary manner.

Unfortunately, certain groups are assumed, rightly or wrongly, to dislike other groups, whether the difference be ethnic, religious, or racial, and this is also taken into account when the time to exercise the peremptory challenge arrives.

A person with some knowledge of the field involved in the trial is a dangerous juror in the lawyer's view. He holds himself out as a fully qualified expert in the jury room, disregarding the evidence and the arguments of the other jurors. People in this category are usually professional people, their spouses, and experts in certain non-legal fields.

It is felt by many lawyers that people of the artistic or entertainment world, waitresses, waiters, and bartenders usually favor the plaintiff civilly and the defendant criminally. They are supposedly realists and worldly-wise, quick to overlook a minor fault by a human being. In civil cases, the same applies to policemen and firemen.

People who are usually for the defendant in civil cases and for the prosecution in criminal cases are retired military men (coming from a strict, non-excusing background), civil servants, men in the insurance industry, and farmers.

It must be stressed most emphatically that these are only generalizations and are subject to more exceptions than can be imagined. Quite often, these opinions are untrue. No two farmers think exactly alike. Many a waiter has voted for the prosecution. In fact, it has been aptly observed that to decide on a peremptory challenge because of a prospective juror's age, color, religion, or name only, exposes the attorney's prejudices, not the juror's.

These are some of the considerations that solve the riddle of why some jurors are rejected and others retained. Of course, a judge may excuse a juror on his own motion, even if neither counsel has challenged him.

Once a challenge has been made, it cannot be withdrawn, except with respect to a challenge to the array. If the juror is off the jury, he is off for good and may not be recalled for that jury.

Challenges are as old as the common law. In early England, there were laws providing for challenges which were essentially to the array and for cause. Interestingly enough, in civil cases, there were no peremptory challenges permitted. In criminal cases, the defendant was entitled to a huge number of peremptory challenges— thirty-five, or one less than three full juries. Originally the Crown, representatives of the King, had an unlimited number of peremptory challenges, but this privilege was so abused that eventually the right was severely curtailed.

Not every question that pops into a lawyer's mind can be asked of a juror. The general rule is that a juror will not be required to answer any question that would tend to humiliate him or bring him into disrepute, nor can the *voir dire* be used to create prejudice.

There are some questions that are usually asked of the jury as a whole and others that are put to the individual jurors. The attorneys ask if any of the jurors know any of the parties or their attorneys. He may mention the names of certain vital witnesses and inquire whether these people are known to the jury. He delves into whether they or their immediate family have even been involved in similar litigation.

Individual jurors may be questioned as to their place of birth, education, knowledge of the English language, their health and condition of their senses and faculties. Questions are asked as to their previous experience as jurors, anything that would indicate even indirect financial interest in the outcome of the litigation, and as to their marital status. What are the prospective juror's social and fraternal affiliations? Does he have a prejudice against this type of lawsuit or this type of party?

The juror may not be asked the meaning of legal terms to be brought out at the trial, unless the intent of the question is to see if the juror understands English.

Usually, the judge will not allow an "iffy" question to be asked, that is, what would the juror do if certain evidence were brought out at the trial. However, the juror in a criminal case usually can be asked if he would be prejudiced if the defendant did not take the stand to testify.

When jurors are excused, it is usually done with a good deal of courtesy and caution. The rough handling of a rejected juror may prejudice the rest of the panel. Jurors may have become friends in the jury waiting room, and if one is excused, the other might be annoyed at having been separated from his or her new-found lunch partner.

In some jurisdictions, the first juror selected is the foreman of the jury, charged with conducting the deliberation, taking the votes, and delivering the verdict in open court. In other areas, the jury elects its foreman.

Now the challenges have been exercised. Twelve unchallenged persons sit in the jury box. The jury has been selected.

8 The Players and the Ground Rules

IN A SENSE, a trial is a show, highly stylized, with a form or script, though the script may be fluid, the lines unsure and constantly surprising. Looked at in this light, the jury constitutes both the audience and the critics, listening and deciding. A strict examination of the function of the jury, however, would not be complete without an inquiry into the functions of the other participants in the drama, the judge serving as the director of the piece, the lawyers as protagonists, and the witnesses as supporting cast, sometimes stealing the show. The script is comprised of the testimony, and the framework and guidelines for such testimony are known as the rules of evidence.

The man on the bench in his black robes, the judge, directs the entire production. In effect, he runs the trial. He must decide on the myriad complicated questions of law that arise in every trial. He must determine the competency of witnesses. He must maintain the decorum of the courtroom and keep the participants in line and on the path leading to the quickest and fairest disposition of the case. He must inform the jury as to the law. These and a hundred other functions are included in the job of being a judge.

In the Federal courts, judges are appointed for life and are only subject to removal for cause. They are not dependent for their jobs on the vagaries of politics and can be independent in their actions. In the states and cities, most judges are elected, while others are appointed by the governor.

The general rule as to the differing roles of the judge and jury is that the judge decides what law is applicable, while the members of the jury are the triers, or weighers, of the facts.

What is the distinction between law and fact? In plain language, facts are concerned with what happened, what transpired. Law, on the other hand, may be defined as rules set by the legislature or past court decisions, which place a measured effect or consequence on a given set of acts.

There is an overlapping of the duties of a judge and jury under these definitions. The judge must decide on the pertinency of a "fact" and decide whether a witness or written evidence is competent, that is, if it may be accepted as admissible evidence. He determines whether the jury may have such "evidence" submitted to it at all. He can dismiss a case without letting the jury decide, if he feels there is an insufficiency of evidence. In effect, he weighs the evidence in almost the same way a juror does. The jury's province is to rule on the validity of admitted evidence, the inferences to be drawn from testimony and the credibility of witnesses.

Lawyers are an indispensable part of the trial system as well. They are bound by many restrictions in their dealings with the courts, their clients, and the public at large. The lawyer is considered an officer of the court and is bound by its orders. In dealing with clients, he must exercise the highest degree of integrity, honesty, and fair dealing. He must obey his client's instructions unless they conflict with the law or with the Code of Ethics set by each state which regulates the conduct of lawyers.

At the trial, attorneys decide the manner of proof, the order of calling witnesses. They argue before the judge with respect to the many points of law that come up in a trial, and attempt to convince the jury of the justice of their clients' positions. They cannot decide the guilt or innocence of a client. The judge and jury do the deciding.

The witnesses are the ones the jurors listen to in determining the facts for themselves. A witness is one who can testify at a trial so as to shed material light on the issues at hand. Witnesses may appear voluntarily or may be subpoenaed, and there are basically two types, the ordinary witness, who can testify as to the facts involved in the case, and expert witnesses.

Though not physically present at a trial, a witness may testify through the means of a deposition, primarily used in civil cases. At some time before trial, his testimony is transcribed and sworn to. This use of depositions is a relatively new concept, being unknown under the common law, the law of old England. The uses of such depositions vary widely from state to state.

Who may testify as a witness? Any person can do so in both criminal and civil cases, unless such person is held to be incompetent by common law or a pertinent statute. Even a judge can testify as to any facts within his knowledge if he disqualifies himself from presiding over that specific trial. Other officers of the court may testify, and, unless the particular state has passed a statute forbidding it (and many have), a sitting juror may testify. Lawyers may testify in a case, even on behalf of their own client, but under those circumstances, they should have another lawyer actually try the case.

Common law disqualified many people from testifying, and today's laws, although modified, do the same. Insane persons under the common law and in most states today are incompetent as witnesses. At common law, people who were deaf and dumb, who had been convicted of infamous crimes, such as treason or murder, and of crimes involving some element of fraud, such as perjury or counterfeiting, were incompetent to testify. Today, however, they are allowed to testify in most states, but the jury may decide what weight, if any, is to be given their testimony.

Child witnesses can testify, but there is always a problem as to how much credence the jury should give to their testimony. Does the child realize what he is testifying to, and its importance? The common law prescribed no age below which children could not testify, although some authorities on legal history believe that a youngster of over fourteen was presumed to be competent and one under seven was presumed incompetent. But no flat rule can be set. The best compromise that has been reached is to allow the judge to question the child and use his judicial discretion to determine his competency to testify.

These are ordinary witnesses, those who can throw light on the proceedings because of facts that they personally know. Occasionally there comes before the jury a different type of witness, the expert witness. Actually the category is divided into two parts, the skilled and expert witness. A skilled witness is one possessed of some special knowledge and can testify as to his own observations and opinions based thereon. Examples of skilled witnesses are accountants who make summaries of entries from a complicated set of commercial account books, experienced construction men and builders with reference to their particular fields, experts on damage to property, crime detection, identity and foreign laws, and the value of personal and other services.

The true expert witness, however, can testify as to his opinion based upon certain facts, no matter how those facts were obtained. Such category may include handwriting experts, experts on engineering, chemistry, and physics. In a sense, all expert opinion invades the province of the jury, since the expert witness is drawing conclusions from facts, the actual job of a jury.

There are times when the jury may want to know about a conversation between certain individuals that would be germane to the issues, but is prevented from hearing it. Why? As a matter of public policy it has been recognized from earliest times that in certain relationships there should be permitted discussion that need not be revealed—what is called a privileged or confidential communication. Under certain circumstances, such privilege may be waived, but there are still instances where it applies.

At common law there was granted such a right of refusal to testify when the privileged confidential communication had taken place between a husband and wife or between a client and his attorney. Today, with regard to husbands and wives, each state has a different rule, but the privilege has in good part been removed. It is now limited to truly confidential communications, when no one else was present, although if an eavesdropper overheard the conversation, it could be repeated as testimony. As to attorneys and their clients, the communication today must have been imparted in strict confidence, must refer to legitimate matters and be related to the client's case in order for the privilege of refusing to testify to apply.

Today, there is a doctor-patient privilege as to confidential communications, although there was no such privilege at common law. Confidential communications between priests and penitents were not privileged at common law either, but most states today have passed laws making them privileged.

Grand jurors must not divulge the details of their deliberations, except by court order, and the same is true for petit jurors, unless there is an official inquiry into possible fraud and corruption. National defense secrets are privileged, unless the government itself institutes a criminal proceeding in which such evidence becomes relevant.

Such are the participants, their roles, rights, and duties. Now they are all gathered in the courtroom, together with the jury, to see, hear, and give evidence, evidence from which a decision will be drawn. The jury, however, is not entitled to hear everything that a witness cares to tell it. Certain rules of evidence have been established that have severely curtailed what may be imparted to the panel.

The ancients thought there was need for such rules of evidence. During the time that jurors were changing from witnesses with personal knowledge to triers of facts presented to them by others, judges had to begin to rule on what juries could hear. Today there is a formally and fully accepted body of rules as to what evidence is admissible in a trial.

A complete rendition of the rules of evidence could fill a rather large book by itself, but let us observe, in general, what the jury may hear, what it may not hear—and why.

There are various classifications of evidence. Testimony is oral evidence given by a witness under oath. Documentary evidence is in the form of writings. Direct evidence is some form of the above types of evidence that will directly go to prove a fact at issue, such as "I saw him stab the deceased." Circumstantial evidence is evidence of one fact that will lead to the implying of another fact, such as "The victim was on the ground and I saw the defendant standing over him, a bloody knife in his hand." This leads from the fact as testified to the conclusion that the standing man had stabbed the victim, although the witness did not actually see this happen. Real evidence is a thing or person exhibited to the jury.

In the movies and on television, the hero-lawyer always leaps to his feet and objects that the question is "irrelevant, incompetent, and immaterial." True enough, evidence must be relevant, competent (not barred by any rule excluding it), and material (another facet of "relevant," but stronger).

The general rule is that all evidence that is relevant shall be admissible, except if there is an exclusionary rule. It can be seen, therefore, that the rules of evidence are mostly made up of rules of exclusion.

With regard to circumstantial evidence, it is admissible if it is relevant to an issue in the case. This is not a matter of law; it is one of logic. The fact that the knife mentioned earlier was bloody is circumstantial and relevant; the fact that the handle was blue is circumstantial and irrelevant, unless you are trying to establish the identity of the knife itself. If the relevancy is too remote or conjectural, the testimony will not be admitted into evidence.

Usually witnesses can only testify to facts, not opinions. This is for the jury to decide. However, expert witnesses can give opinions within their own field.

One of the most basic exceptions to the rule favoring admissibility of evidence is the hearsay rule. In short, this is the repeating of someone else's statement, such statement having been made out of court. For example, "I was told by a witness to the accident that the plaintiff was speeding." The jury may wonder why this would be excluded. But the missing witness cannot be cross-examined, and such a third-party statement is usually not made under oath, as testimony at the trial would be.

Of course, there are exceptions to the hearsay rule. They become quite complex, but such exceptions may involve voluntary confessions, the declarations of dying persons, statements uttered at the time of an accident, and so forth.

Other important phases of the laws of evidence include the rules defining the limits of contracts, and the rule requiring that if a party seeks to prove the contents of a writing, he must produce the original or satisfactorily account for its absence.

These are not all the rules of evidence, but a general picture can be obtained of a system hard at work trying to get truthful answers to the questions at issue. The jurors usually do not know of these rules, and so may be puzzled by the exclusion of evidence they would like to hear. Still, the system is the fairest one to all sides that has yet been devised.

9 Target: the Jury

THE PRELIMINARIES are over. The jury is selected. The judge is ready. It is time for the trial.

At the front of the courtroom is a raised bench, behind which the judge sits. Off to one side is an enclosed area, containing the jury box, in which the jury sits while listening to the testimony. In front of the judge's bench usually stand two tables, one for each of the opposing attorneys. Next to the judge's bench, and between it and the jury box, is a solitary chair. This will be the center of all eyes in the days to come, the witness stand.

Now the jury must be sworn, agreeing to fairly try the issues. This is usually done in the presence of the parties involved and in open court. The jury rises, raise their right hands and the oath is read to them, to which they then respond and swear by saying, "I do."

After a jury has been selected, approved by the respective attorneys, and sworn, the court may not, without the consent of both parties, discharge a juror except for good cause, such as an emergency involving sickness or an accident. If such discharge of a juror is made before the evidence has begun to unfold, a replacement may be chosen by the original jury-selection method, or a whole new jury may be picked. If the trial has begun at all, no substitution may be made without the consent of the parties, for otherwise the trial must begin all over again. Sometimes the parties agree that if a juror is to be dropped, a verdict may be reached by the eleven remaining jurors, or however many are left.

Basically, taking the trial of a civil action as an example, there are six stages in the proceeding.

First, the respective lawyers make their opening statements of what they intend to prove. Second, the plaintiff's lawyer, representing the person suing, calls his witnesses and produces his evidence. He is usually under a duty to produce all his evidence before he closes, uninterrupted except for cross-examination. The judge, however, has wide powers of discretion in varying the usual order of proof, even on occasion calling the jury back from its deliberations at the end of the trial to hear new evidence (although this is extremely rare).

What does the plaintiff have to prove in this hypothetical civil action? Assume it is an accident case in which the plaintiff, a driver of one car, was struck by the defendant's car that allegedly passed a red light, causing the plaintiff to sustain personal injuries.

The plaintiff will testify as to the details of the accident: time, place, circumstances of his route, and the physical layout of the place of occurrence. His lawyer, through questioning, will elicit the fact that he was driving on one street, that when he reached the corner he had the green light in his favor, that he saw the defendant driving down the cross street, pass the red light, and hit him. He did everything that a reasonable man could do to avoid the accident, but the defendant drove in such a manner that the accident occurred anyway.

The plaintiff will thereafter testify as to what parts of his body were injured, the extent of hospital and medical treatment he received, and the time he lost from work as a result of his injuries. If there is a hospital record, it is put into evidence so that the jury will know what injuries he was treated for at the hospital and what that treatment consisted of. If there was a private treating physician, he will be called to the stand to testify as to the injuries, his treatment, the amount of his bill, and the outlook for the plaintiff's recovery.

If there are other witnesses to be used for corroboration or to further prove items of liability or damage, these, too, will be called by the plaintiff's attorney.

After he has questioned each witness so as to bring out his story to the jurors, the defendant's attorney may cross-examine to try to impeach the story as untrue, or even attack the credibility of the witness himself.

In attempting to attack such testimony, questions may be asked as to the sharpness of a witness' senses, such as that of a man who is required to wear eyeglasses at all times, but was not wearing them at the time he claims he saw an accident occur half a block away. The witness may be interrogated and tested as to his ability to remember details, and with regard to inconsistencies between his present story and statements given by him previously.

Certainly, the witness may be asked as to his relationship to or friendship with the party on whose behalf he is testifying. When cross-examination is concluded, the plaintiff's attorney may ask further questions in an attempt to rehabilitate the original testimony.

When the plaintiff's attorney has finished calling his witnesses, it is time for the third step, the defendant's turn. The defendant's attorney leads his witnesses through their stories, following which they are subjected to cross-examination.

In the fourth step, rebuttal, witnesses may be called or recalled to disprove the opposition's contentions.

The fifth step consists of the closing arguments addressed to the jury by the lawyers on both sides. Lastly, the judge instructs the jury as to what law applies to the case at hand.

During the course of the trial, motions may be made by either lawyer as to points of law, and the judge rules on them. Many objections are also raised as to procedure, propriety of questions, and the like, and these, too, the judge will rule on.

As can be seen, the three occasions when the participants are directing themselves exclusively to the jury are the opening statements, the closing statements (or summations, as they are called), and the giving of instructions by the judge to the jury. Let us examine these vital segments of the trial in some detail.

The opening to the jury is actually a statement made by counsel in which he informs them of the facts he intends to prove in order to establish the charge or right of action.

The jury is apprised of the substance of the questions involved in the lawsuit. This enables the jury, even before hearing any evidence, to understand in a general way what to look for and to view the items of evidence as pieces of a jigsaw puzzle which will fit together to form a complete picture. The plaintiff usually has the advantage of opening first, and also of summing up last, since he has the burden of proof in the action.

After the plaintiff has completed his opening, the defendant will quite often deliver an opening, outlining his defense and thus enabling the jurors to watch for holes in the testimony presented by the plaintiff that would tend to confirm the defendant's story. Sometimes this opening by the defendant may be deferred until the end of the plaintiff's case.

The old-time English opening was practically the entire case in itself. Not only did the plaintiff deliver the full extent of his claim and an outline of the evidence to be produced, but he was required to give a recitation of the legal grounds for support of his position, remarks in anticipation of the expected defenses to be raised by the defendant, and reasons why such defenses were futile. This occupied many hours, and even days, and it all occurred before one shred of evidence was heard!

The opening in England today, while longer than our openings, is severely curtailed, constituting a statement of the facts and some preliminary argument. Under their system, the defendant makes his opening after all of the plaintiff's evidence is in.

In present-day America, both sides have an absolute

right to make an opening statement to the jury, but the opening is little more than a statement of the facts intended to be proven. There is no detailed recitation of the evidence of each witness, nor a lengthy reading of any documentary evidence. If the lawyer steps outside reasonable bounds in his opening, the court may curtail his speech.

In many jurisdictions, including the Federal courts, photographs and charts may be used in the opening, if assurance is given that such items can be properly authenticated.

During the course of the opening, the adversary may object to any statement that he feels is irrelevant, incompetent, or misleading. The judge will rule on the objection and if it is upheld (sustained), the judge will instruct the jury to ignore it.

No rule prevents eloquence or the use of forensic arts in the opening. In fact, among the best trial lawyers are those who are, in effect, good actors and speechmakers. Practically any and all verbal weapons have been tried in an effort to capture the jury's minds and imaginations. This is, of course, even more true of the summation at the end of the case.

The trick is to attract the jury's attention to what will follow. In a recent case where an allegedly stolen car hit the plaintiff's vehicle, the plaintiff followed the offending vehicle through a trail of gasoline it had left when its gas tank was damaged. The trail led to the car which was parked directly in front of the owner's house! The defendant had contended from the very beginning of the lawsuit that the car had been stolen and consequently that he was not liable for any damage caused by his auto while driven by the thief.

Knowing the facts as to where the trail had led, the plaintiff's lawyer, in his opening, dubbed the action as "The Case of the Thoughtful Thief." Laying down a bare outline of the facts, the plaintiff's attorney then let the evidence itself reveal the details and the further fact that the defendant had two teen-age sons living with him. At the end of the trial, the lawyer then struck home with the point as to what thief would be considerate enough to return a stolen car to the very door of the owner from whom it had been taken. It was intimated rather strongly that it must have been the teen-age sons who had taken the car out on a joy ride. After a short deliberation, the jury awarded the plaintiff a substantial recovery. Some of the jurors said afterwards that the title given to the case had held their interest and they eagerly awaited any evidence to show why the "Thief" had been called "Thoughtful," and that this was a decisive factor in their deliberations.

Examples are rife of lawyers being fooled by the apparent interest of a particular juror in their arguments, only to find that such juror was the only one to vote against them.

This situation, plus a natural mistake, once led to a classic comedy of errors. One of New York's finest trial attorneys was trying an accident case. Being a trial specialist, he was trying the case for another lawyer who was not experienced in trial work. He had seen the client only once before, quite some time before this day in court.

In his opening to the jury, this lawyer noted that juror number four was nodding his head vigorously at everything that the lawyer said. He thought, "If he's on my side already, now at the very beginning, this case is as good as won!" At that moment, the original attorney walked into the courtroom, looked at the jury box and turned pale. In a choked voice, he whispered, "Mr. Green, what are you doing in the jury box?"

Juror number four was the plaintiff.

It developed that he had walked into the courtroom early, had seen an empty chair in the jury box and had sat down. This was understandable, but where was the real juror number four? He was discovered in the back of the courtroom, looking sheepish. Since all twelve chairs in the jury box had been occupied when he came in, he took any seat he could find.

The summation, or closing statement, is the second occasion when the jurors are addressed directly. Coming at the end of all the evidence, it performs a dual function. First, it serves as a method whereby all the bits and pieces of evidence are gathered into meaningful pictures, albeit sometimes entirely different pictures as shown by the opposing attorneys. Secondly, it allows the opposing lawyers to argue as to who has the better right to a favorable verdict, the arguments being sometimes heated, sometimes coldly precise, but always designed to be persuasive.

The summation may include a discussion of the issues that have emerged at the trial, the credibility of witnesses, the probability of testimony given as weighed and fitted in with all the other evidence brought forth.

The right to speak last to the jury is both valuable and vital. Arguments presented then can no longer be answered by the person who closed first. In addition, the last words heard by a person before deciding anything are usually most persuasive and likely to be remembered.

The length of the closing may be restricted by the court, but this is usually done only if the attorneys are extremely long-winded and repetitious. Certain states, however, do not trust the judge to limit the speeches and they have passed statutes setting time limits.

Summation is the art of oratory intertwined with a search for justice and truth. No two lawyers will sum up in the same way. The plaintiff's attorney will attempt to show that he has met the burden of proof. The arguments by both attorneys usually are vigorous, may be dramatic, and are sometimes illustrated by personal incidents.

During the course of a trial, the attorneys may indirectly appeal to the emotions of a jury, and this is done quite often not only by words but by deeds. The defendant's tearful wife and squalling babies may be sitting in the front row of the spectators' section of the courtroom, or the lawyer may put his arm around the defendant's shoulders during summation, so that the jury may infer and remember that the defendant, too, is a human being, subject to the same frailties as they.

As a general rule, decisions in similar cases or legal texts may not be read to the jury, although a statute on which the defense or recovery is based can quite often be read.

Can the jury take notes during the trial and use them during the deliberations? In the absence of a statute, the judge may permit them to do so. Suppose a case involves an interminable amount of figures. Note-taking here may be a good thing. In the average case, however, the industrious juror does not take full notes of all the evidence and, the human mind being what it is, he will tend to stress the points during deliberation that he wrote down, to the detriment of equally important facts that he failed to note because they did not penetrate his awareness at the time or even because his nose itched at just that moment. In general, note-taking is not allowed.

In criminal cases, the summations may include a discussion of the penalty by the lawyers, to let the jury know what they will be dooming the defendant to by a verdict of "guilty." In civil cases, the nature and extent of the claim or injury can be discussed, and most states allow the amount of money sought to be mentioned. In support of the claim, the factors of permanency of the injury, future ability to earn a living, disfigurement, pain, and suffering will be stressed. The defendant, on the other hand, will claim that the plaintiff himself either caused or contributed to the event in question. He will attempt to minimize the items of damage. Expert testimony, such as that of a doctor, is translated into everyday terms by the lawyers in summation.

In civil cases, the request by the plaintiff's lawyer for a specific amount by way of damages raises problems. How is it possible to measure adequately repayment for pain and suffering? If it were exactitude that was sought, it would be impossible. The guidelines that the jury must use in determining such a question are usually left to the courts in their reasonable administration of justice.

The courts are divided as to whether a formula for damages may be cited to the jury. Those against it say it is an unwarranted assumption and an invasion of the jury's rights. Those for it say it is a mere suggested means of reasonable compensation, and does not invade the province of the jury. Most states permit the plaintiff's lawyer to name a flat amount requested, since it is only a suggestion to the jury. In a few jurisdictions only, the defendant's lawyer may point out that a recovery for an injury is not subject to Federal income taxation.

Quite often, one fact in the case, if properly stressed, may become the crucial turning point in summation. But the closing statement is not always limited to words. A legendary story that has circulated among lawyers for many years is that of a case in which the defendant was accused of poisoning another person. The balance of the poison, in a bottle, was placed in evidence and rested on the counsel table. The defendant's attorney picked up the bottle, gazed at the jury, and said, "I will show you how certain I am that this is not poison." He then gulped down the contents of the bottle. While the jury, duly impressed, retired and found a verdict of "not guilty," the attorney rushed across the street and had his stomach pumped out. Knowing that it was a slow-acting poison, he had arranged in advance for the medical apparatus to be made ready.

The third time juries are directly addressed is when the judge charges the jury as to the law applicable to the case.

There are two reasons for such a charge or statement from the judge. The first is to define the issues for the jurors and the steps they are to take in determining these issues. The second is to apprise any appeals court as to the trial judge's view of the questions that arose in the case, and what law applies to these issues.

Such charges were known to the earliest English courts for which we have records. At that time, the judge also summed up the evidence for the jury and expressed an opinion on it. Our Federal courts do something quite similar today, but the judge is careful to point out that the jury is not bound by his opinions, only as to his determinations of what laws apply to the issues in the case.

Many states require written instructions from the judge to the jury. In some states, such instructions are submitted by opposing counsel and the judge takes his choice. Other states specify that the judge draw up his own charge in writing, although he may accept suggestions from the lawyers in the case. Still other states only require that the charge be delivered orally to the jury, without it having been reduced to writing.

There are certain elements of a charge that are fairly standard in all states. The judge identifies the parties and then states their respective claims and defenses. Based upon this, he sets forth the issues raised and, under the pertinent rules of law, what the jury must find in order for either party to win a verdict in its favor. He then explains the steps necessary in such determination, the rules of law and evidence applicable, and the effect of his denial of any motions made by the lawyers during the course of the trial.

The judge cautions against sympathy or prejudice. Further cautionary statements that he may make deal with specific circumstances, such as that an indictment is just an accusation and is no proof of guilt; that the jury has no right to disregard the evidence; and the fact that if the judge charges as to the measure of damages, this is no indication that he feels that damages should be awarded.

If the defendant in a criminal case has not taken the stand, the judge should charge the jury that the defendant, under the Fifth Amendment to the Constitution whereby a man does not have to be a witness against himself, has a right to refuse to so testify, and that no adverse inference may be drawn from this fact.

In a civil case, he will charge that if damages are to be awarded, how those damages are to be computed. In all cases he states what form the verdict must take: in a civil case, either for the plaintiff in a certain amount, or for the defendant; in a criminal case, either "not guilty," or "guilty" and the degree of guilt (such as "guilty of murder in the first degree") that may be found.

As to the questions he presents to the jury for determination, the judge will find them in the issues created by the pleadings and sustained by the evidence. He, of course, must state where the burden of proof lies. The judge will charge that the weight of the proof is not to be measured by the number of witnesses called by each side but by the quality, or believability, of their testimony.

Though the testimony of a witness be uncontradicted, the weight to be given to such testimony remains with the jury.

When reaching the section of the charge dealing with the applicable law the judge will cite the statutes and the holdings that have arisen from earlier and similar cases. His instructions constitute the law of that particular case and the jury is bound by it. They have no right to disregard it or to substitute their own notions of right and wrong. This sounds fine in theory, but there is no real way to prevent a jury from doing just that. In fact, it is not certain that it should be prevented, since the action of these twelve may represent more closely the "conscience of the community" than a possibly antiquated law.

For instance, there was a widespread rejection in the seventeenth, eighteenth, and nineteenth centuries of the common law rule in England that all convicted murderers were subject to a mandatory sentence of death.

This rejection of the rules of law might be quite valid in the case where a husband has slain his wife's lover, but it can be carried to an excess of laxity, as in the recent case in New Mexico where a nineteen-year-old boy who had admitted taking a car without the consent of the owner was found not guilty, presumably on the theory of giving him a second chance.

If there are legal or technical terms that have been used in the trial, they will be explained by the judge. For instance, "contract" has a very definite legal meaning, which the layman may not have been acquainted with before, and so does "negligence."

In some states, the judge will state his opinion as to the credibility of the witnesses; in all states he will give to the jury the factors to use in determining such credibility. Some such considerations to be taken into account are appearance and demeanor while testifying; the witness' apparent intelligence and opportunity to have observed what he described; his interest, motive or lack of same in the outcome of the case; the degree of probability of his testimony and whether there was any corroboration for it. If the jury finds a witness has lied, they will be charged that they can disregard his entire testimony or the part they believe to be untrue.

In charging as to damages in civil cases, the judge will point out that the jury may only consider admitted evidence. Conjecture will not be allowed. Whatever has been proved by way of expenses (medical and other), lost earnings, past and future pain and suffering and permanency may be considered. For example, if no proof was properly adduced as to the amount of a hospital bill, this cannot be included in damages.

With regard to opposing counsel's summation and arguments, some jurisdictions permit the court to comment on them, although the judge must remain fair and dispassionate. In other states, the judge will point out that such attorney's statements are not evidence, but he is not permitted to tell the jury to disregard them entirely.

The judge may not coerce a jury into agreeing to a verdict by stating that when a vote is taken, the minority should give in to the majority.

Technically, the judge should be impartial as much in

his tone of voice as in his words. Everything should be clearly and accurately stated and be relevant to the issues presented by the pleadings and evidence. He must state the law correctly, even if he only paraphrases a statute, instead of reading the entire text of it. He must not dwell on one point to such an extent that it will make an undue impression in the minds of the jurors.

Once again, this is nice in theory, but judges are human, too, and also have opinions on how the case should be decided. Quite often, therefore, you will find the judge accenting certain portions by voice alone, or occasionally repeating a certain part of the charge in a strong voice. There is no question but that the jury understands his point, but it is surprising how often it asserts its independence and ignores an attempt to direct its findings.

What if the judge has made an error and it is called to his attention after the jury has retired or, further, if he wishes to give additional instructions? Many states have statutes governing this situation, but in the absence of any such law, the judge may call the jury back into the courtroom and instruct the jury further. Counsel for both sides must be present at this time.

At last it is all done and the jury retires to the jury room to consider its verdict. No further words can avail either side. It is now in the hands of the twelve and the jury must perform the duty it was created for.

10   Deliberation

Now THEY ARE left alone. They were selected from the masses, they have been questioned, examined, their lives pried into; they have been flattered, cajoled, instructed as to the law. Now there is no longer anyone to help them. The facts are theirs. The decision is theirs.

The facts upon which the jury must render a decision must come from the evidence presented. Of course, this does not mean that the juryman has to leave his common sense and knowledge of the community and the world at the threshold of the jury room.

As an illustration, a man in New York claimed that his suit had been ruined through the negligence of the defendant. "A brand new suit," he cried, and he wanted the full price of it. In the jury room a consumer-wise housewife, playing the detective before the rest of the obviously uninformed male jurors, turned the lining of the sleeve out. She knew that the cleaners in that particular community marked the inside of the sleeve any time a suit was cleaned or pressed. Sure enough, there were the cleaners' marks, many of them. The jury acted accordingly and the plaintiff never knew why the jury didn't accept his story of a "new" suit.

Obtaining the facts from the evidence means that anything pertaining to the case at hand that is revealed to the jurors outside of such boundaries is improper and may cause not only reversal of the verdict or a mistrial, but may, under certain circumstances, subject the imparter of such opinion or knowledge to criminal prosecution. Of course, if substantial justice was meted out to the parties involved or if the additional information was innocuous, the verdict will not be reversed. A verdict is a hardy creature, and it takes a good deal of error to reverse it.

Many items imparted to the jurors are made in good faith, though nonetheless improper. In Illinois, a witness, after testifying and while getting off the witness stand, confided confidentially to the twelve in the box that he hoped they would do the right thing by the plaintiff.

Jurors do not live in the courtroom. They are ordinary citizens who eat in restaurants, walk through the courthouse corridors, and live in homes. It has been held that if there is a discussion outside the courtroom between a witness and a juror, this is usually subject to reversal of the verdict by a higher court. The same is true if the second person in the conversation with the juror is one of the parties or an attorney. Does this mean that one can't say "Good morning" to a juror? Certainly not. If the conversation is brief and not involving the case, it is usually considered to be harmless. Many is the lawyer, however, who walks through the court corridors with his eyes down so as not to have to snub a juror he may meet.

The jury is not even supposed to speak to third persons, unless it is a court officer. Of course, this rule is difficult to enforce, but a juror is supposed to report to the judge if anyone has attempted to speak to him about the case.

The rule is sometimes carried to extremes, as in the holding that jurors should not even discuss the action among themselves before retiring or express an opinion on the case. There is a good reason for this. If the jurors do so, they may tend to stress certain facets as they are raised, instead of looking at the evidence as a whole at the end of the trial. Once again, however, if it is found that jurors have disobeyed this rule, it will usually be held to have been harmless and the verdict will not be disturbed.

As there are improper conversations, so there is improper conduct. It has been known, especially years ago, for liquor, bought and paid for by a party in the case, to be smuggled to the jurors, a proper "thank you" verdict being expected. Some unscrupulous parties or lawyers have arranged to be at the restaurants or other public places where it is known a juror will be, offering an outright promise of "benefits" (usually monetary) if the juror will vote "the right way."

Jurors are sometimes guilty of improper conduct, though it may be brought about by the best of intentions. There have been numerous instances of eager-beaver jurors who, during the course of the trial, will run to the library during recess and look up books on particular subjects involved at the trial. Thus, with an incomplete knowledge of the subject, he will appear as the "expert" in the jury room and wrongfully influence his colleagues.

Sometimes the description of the scene of the occurrence of an accident leaves questions in the mind of a juror and he goes to visit the place. Once again, this is forbidden. It is even silly. After all, quite often the case is coming up for trial many months or even years after the incident and the physical layout may have changed. A "full stop" sign may have been replaced by a traffic light; a building may have been erected on the corner, thus obstructing a view that was previously unobstructed. Unless it can be shown, however, that such an unauthorized viewing incorrectly influenced the jury, such a visit will be deemed to be harmless.

Criminal trials get the big play in the newspapers. Unlike England, where very little is permitted to be exposed by the information media prior to a verdict, the American newspapers are full of running accounts of sensational trials, sidelights of the case that will never get into evidence, and the paper's opinions on the evidence presented. It is highly improper for a juror to read such accounts, though he may be most curious. To reverse a verdict because a juror has done this, however, a lawyer must show specific prejudice arising from this breach of conduct, a most difficult thing to do.

In early common-law England, jurors were pariahs, untouchable, kept together and segregated from their fellow citizens from the time they were sworn till the time they reached a verdict. These were usually short trials, however. As the contests grew lengthier, and the decision no longer rested on the personal knowledge of the jurors, this rule was discarded.

America has never had a general rule of keeping the jury together during the entire trial. Why penalize the jurors and keep them from their homes and loved ones? This is not to say that such procedure is never followed. The judge has the discretion to so order it, but such discretion is exercised only in rare instances. One of the most frequent occasions when the judge will keep such a jury together is in a criminal trial where the prejudice of the community against the defendant is apparent to one and all.

After the jury has been charged as to the law and deliberation begins, they are usually kept together. Who is the jury's keeper? The court usually names some official person, such as a court clerk, a marshal, or a deputy. There has even been an instance of a witness being named as guardian over the jury during its deliberations. This guardian preserves the jury's immunity from contact with the outside world, shepherds them to meals, and performs other similar functions.

The jury is not the only thing that goes into the jury room. At common law, with rare exceptions, no documents were allowed to be in the jury room during deliberation. The general rule today is that all exhibits that were properly admitted into evidence may be taken in with the jury, as was the "new" suit referred to earlier. Exhibits may include pictures, maps, and other explanatory papers, as well as physical objects such as liquor, guns, or diamonds. Sometimes items not in evidence, things used for illustrative purposes only, such as a map of an intersection, may be given to the jury.

Many states permit the pleadings, the charges, and defenses prepared by the lawyers at the very beginning of the lawsuit to be taken in with the jury to the deliberation room. Possibly the better view is that of those states that do not allow this, since such pleadings are mere allegations and are not proof of anything.

Depositions, or examinations before trial, as they are sometimes called, are not permitted into deliberations in most states, and rightfully so. As in the case of note-taking by jurors, this would be something concrete they could re-read and would weigh unduly as compared with the testimony that had to be remembered. In addition, unless introduced into evidence, the jury may not take into its deliberations any law books, tomes on medicine, or similar volumes.

What does the jury do with these exhibits in their seclusion? In most cases, the jurors attend strictly to business and examine the items. Alas, though, jurors are human, too, and although such instances are few in number, there has been a case in practically every jurisdiction where a full bottle of whiskey, admitted into evidence and taken into the jury room, has been found quite empty after verdict. Rather lamely, it might be argued that the jury fully digested the evidence. In one case, a juror lit up some opium that was an exhibit, ostensibly to see if it would burn.

As Shakespeare said:

> The jury, passing on the prisoner's life,
> May in the sworn twelve have a thief or two
> Guiltier than him they try.

While recalling the human frailties of some jurymen, let us step aside from the main trial and see what arrangements are made for the comfort of these twelve. At old common law, it was not a pleasant experience to be a juror. "No food, drink, or candle" was to be provided the jurors until a verdict was reached.

Today, we are more "civilized." The county usually pays for meals for jurors, although in some jurisdictions the contestants in the case split the bills. One party, however, cannot cater the entire feast, for obvious reasons.

Don't think that jurors don't look forward to a free meal. In one case, involving important questions and a good deal of money, the judge had finished charging the jury and, as the jury arose to retire, the lone woman juror indicated she had a question, a rare occurrence. This was a woman who had listened intently to all the testimony, so the judge and both counsel, not to mention the parties, strained forward eagerly to see what was so pressing on her mind. In a vitalized voice, she fervently asked the judge, "Do we still get a free lunch even though we decide before noon?"

Jurors and judges are quite aware of the conditions under which they attend the trial and the deliberations. A certain amount of pride is involved, as befits the performance of a civic duty. In Flint, Michigan, the jurors recently contributed $25 to the court to buy a new flag.

In January, 1970, a New York City judge rebelled against the jury room being kept in such a filthy condition that the jurors had to stand in the corridors during conferences between the court and the attorneys, so he declared he would hold no more jury trials until such conditions were bettered.

Once retired to the confines of the jury room, the foreman takes charge. It is his duty to preside during the discussion, take votes, act as the spokesman for the jury, and deliver its verdict.

The means of deliberation are completely in the hands of the jury. They may debate in any manner they wish and do whatever they think necessary, within reason, to reach a verdict.

In the revelations by a juror in a criminal case, published in October of 1968, the juror summed up what must be the feelings of most jurors—that is, she suddenly realized that she was, in effect, "playing God," that she wished it were "just a game" instead of deciding as to a person's liberty, but that the juror at the end accepted the responsibility and rendered a verdict consonant with the evidence.

Sometimes, stubborn people being the same the world over, a verdict cannot be reached. This was not allowed at common law. The jury could not be released until they did reach a verdict.

Today, the jury can be discharged without rendering a verdict under certain circumstances. If they fail to agree within a reasonable time and they report that there is very little likelihood they will agree (sometimes known as a "hung" or deadlocked jury), the judge will usually disband them and order a new trial for sometime in the future. The same is true if one of the jurors dies or falls gravely ill, or if there is misconduct by one of the twelve.

How long is a reasonable time in which a jury should agree? In the absence of a law or a rule of the court, there is no standard, it resting in the sound discretion of the judge. The mere fact that deliberation has taken a very long time is not sufficient reason to disband the jury. There has to be the additional factor that there is virtually no chance of agreement.

In the event of death or illness on the part of one of the jurors, it may not be necessary to disband the jury if the parties in the case agree that they will consent to a verdict by the remaining jurors.

A slightly better system under these circumstances, in use in the Federal courts and some states, is to have alternate jurors who sit in on the action from the beginning, but do not vote unless they must replace an indisposed juror.

Misconduct of a juror as cause for a mistrial is not what you might think. The misconduct must relate to the case itself and be of a serious nature. The test is as to whether it *could* have influenced the result. Of course, this rule is more stringently observed in criminal cases than in civil cases. In criminal actions, the verdict will usually be set aside unless it is made quite clear that the misconduct was harmless.

Examples of misconduct by jurors are numerous. A juror is biased and concealed this on the *voir dire*. He brings an improper writing into the jury room. He knows about the case of his own knowledge and tells the other jurors about it. He wrongfully communicates with someone outside the jury room during deliberations. Other examples are bribery by a third person, one juror attempting to bribe another to go along with him, or wrongful coercion of one juror by another.

Two means of reaching a verdict are also considered misconduct. Suppose the jury is split, six to six. Up pops Johnny Juror and says, "Let's flip a coin. Heads, he's guilty; tails, he's innocent." No good. A verdict based on this means of decision will be set aside, if later discovered through conversation with the jury.

The second means is the quotient method. A jury in a civil case has run into a deadlock. They can't agree if the plaintiff is entitled to any damages, or if he is, how much. Once again, Johnny Juror says, "Let's write down what each of us thinks the plaintiff should get, add up the figures, and divide by the twelve of us." In theory, this averaging-out may seem like a good idea, but it doesn't work. Suppose eleven say the plaintiff should get nothing, while one says he should get $120,000. By this method, the plaintiff would receive $10,000. With eleven against him, would this quotient method be justice? In addition, the figure usually arrived at by this means is not really the verdict of any one of the jurors. It can be easily discovered, too, since this type of quotient verdict for damages usually winds up as something like $3,932.47, thus bearing no relation to the evidence or the individual opinions of the jurors.

As may be remembered, there can be multiple parties

in a case. This raises problems. If the jury has reached a verdict with respect to one defendant in a criminal case, but cannot agree as to the other, a partial verdict may be rendered, with the defendant on whom no verdict could be reached getting a new trial.

In their deliberations, the jurors must not be disturbed by unauthorized persons. There must be neither interference nor suggestion by anyone, and that includes the judge, court clerk, a party, or his attorney. That is why the jury is placed in the charge of a court officer. He is the guardian at the gate.

If the jury has been deliberating an unusual length of time, the judge may break in to inquire if there is a possibility of agreement. Even the judge, though, may not, as a usual rule, go into the jury room to so quiz the jury, but must call them out into open court.

The be-all and end-all of the jury is the verdict. A Pennsylvania court once said, "No question of fact is too difficult for a modern jury." But the job is not that simple.

There are two types of verdicts, the general and the special verdict. The general verdict is the one best known, the "guilty" or "not guilty" variety. The jury determines all the issues submitted to it and arrives at a general holding in favor of one of the parties.

Sometimes a case is complicated and there are numerous and complex questions of fact. Most states provide in this situation for a special verdict. This means that formalized questions are put to the jury involving the various elements involved in the case, and the jury must answer them one way or the other. Based upon the legal effect of these basic factual findings, the judge then enters a judgment. In some states (Texas, for example) there can be as many as 100 to 150 separate written questions put to the jury.

In the early days of common law, though both general and special verdicts were allowed, there was a valid reason for special verdicts, from the jurors' viewpoint. Frankly, it was because the old-time jurors were cagy. As you may remember, jurors could be found guilty of attaint and penalized if they came in with an erroneous verdict. What simpler system to avoid this could be found than to make findings as to the facts and to permit the judge to render an inescapably-directed judgment based thereon?

The system of special verdicts hung on and was much in use in the colonies. Today, it is still in use in many states in complicated matters, but more modern jurisdictions have abolished them. The Federal courts constitute one of the systems still using the special verdict.

Usually, a state will not permit a jury to return both a general and special verdict. Some areas do, however. In this case, if the findings under the special verdict are inconsistent with the general verdict, the general verdict must be changed.

Juries sometimes try to add reservations and directions to their verdicts. In Alabama in 1868, a jury directed the defendant to pay the judgment in gold. In Minnesota, in 1922, possibly in a spirit of great charity (at someone else's expense) the jury directed the plaintiff to turn the amount recovered over to the Red Cross. In this event, the judge will strike out the superfluous part of the verdict and enter the judgment as corrected.

In many states, where permitted by law, the jurors have the right to determine punishment as well as guilt in capital cases, that is, where death may be the penalty. In six states there are separate trials for guilt and punishment.

Prejudice may raise its head in the verdict. In a survey by Stanford Law School in 1969, it was found that the economic status of defendants in first degree murder cases affected the juries' decisions. Startlingly, in 238 cases analyzed, racial discrimination was not a significant factor.

When the jury returns and the foreman delivers the verdict, how do we know that this actually is the jury's verdict? Could the foreman possibly have made a mistake? The way that this is determined is by polling the jury, that is, asking each juror in open court if that is his verdict. This is allowed in practically every state and, in these states, the right of the losing attorney to have the jury polled is absolute. Of course, in most instances, the poll finds that the verdict as delivered by the foreman is correct, but with regard to the few minutes expended for this procedure, it more than pays for itself in undoing an injustice in those few cases where the requisite amount of juror votes necessary for a verdict have not been obtained.

Juries as a whole can oftentimes make mistakes, too. If there is an inconsistency in the verdict, such as against whom the verdict is to be rendered or as to the amount awarded, the judge will correct the verdict or direct the jury to retire again and do so before it is entered by the clerk of the court. After all, once a jury is discharged, it cannot be recalled to undo a mistake made in its verdict.

Sometimes jurors deliberate to a late hour and when they are ready to render a verdict, lawyers, clerks, stenographers, and even the judge may have gone home. Provision is thus made for a sealed verdict. The verdict is written out, signed, and delivered to the jury's custodian. It is read in open court on the following day. This system is used in most states as the most practical solution to the problem.

Why did the jury decide as it did? Most lawyers would love to know. May the jurors be questioned following the verdict, either to gain insight for the next case or to obtain evidence to set aside the verdict because of the hidden misconduct of a juror?

The general rule, reaching back to England, is that the testimony of a juror may not be received to prove his misconduct or that of his colleagues in reaching a verdict. The basis for this rule is that jurors should not be subjected to the pressure of public disclosure of what occurred in the jury room, thus effectively preserving the integrity of the jury.

To prove impropriety, a fully independent source is necessary, such as a witness who observed jurors at the scene in question during the course of a trial.

Some Federal courts do permit partial interrogation of jurors, but only as to overt acts, such as visiting the scene or the interference with the jury by a third person, such as the bailiff.

Thus is the destiny of the jury fulfilled; the verdict has been reached. Brought together from every imaginable walk of life to fulfill one function, it disbands. This living, vibrant entity, speaking as one, speaks, and then breaks into its component parts, the citizen, each going his separate way.

But it has done its duty and guaranteed its place in our way of life as one of the most important rights enunciated by the Constitution of the United States of America.

11   Around the World

How HAS THE JURY FARED outside the borders of this country? The answer is mixed.

In the nineteenth century, there was a wave of liberal feeling which resulted in the adoption of the jury system by many countries. The impetus to change the old judicial system of despot-appointed judges highhandedly rendering decisions was engendered as a by-product of the French Revolution.

In France, prior to 1789, criminal charges were tried by judges alone, the trials being conducted in secret. This procedure was a direct descendant of the Inquisition, and resulted in great injustice and the frequent use of torture. Thus this system became one of the great concerns in the minds of the people prior to the overthrow of the French monarchy. In 1789, the leaders of the French Revolution demanded the introduction of trial by jury in criminal cases and the Constituent Assembly so established the system in September of 1791. It survived through all the upheavals in government that followed, through the consulate, the empire and, eventually, the republic, though

116

the French jury system developed differently from the common-law, Anglo-American system.

In 1808, Napoleon, seeing the jury as a weapon against the entrenched old aristocracy, firmly championed it. In fact, he attempted to bring its benefits to the countries he conquered.

Most of the states in Germany had adopted the jury system by 1848, and the entire German empire accepted it in 1877. In Prussia, however, those accused of political offenses could not avail themselves of trial by jury. The majority of Swiss cantons, with their inherent love of democracy, avidly accepted it. Spain tried it for a short while prior to 1875, suppressed it out of fear of the increased power of the people, but was forced to restore it in 1888.

Norway, one of the first countries in ancient history to employ a form of the jury, and later to abandon it, held out until 1887, at which time it was again adopted. Most of the Latin American countries went along with the general trend and introduced the jury into their own jurisdictions. Belgium underwent the change in 1830, after it had separated from Holland, and Greece did likewise in 1834. So, too, did Portugal in 1832.

Fighting the trend of that time was The Netherlands, which never adopted a jury system at all in the nineteenth century, and Austria, which abolished trial by jury throughout the Empire in 1852.

The spread of the jury system in Europe and Latin America in the 1800's is surprising in view of the despotic nature of the rulers of these countries. Perhaps it can be said that the mighty oaks were forced to bend by the constant winds of an awakening populace. Russia is a case in point.

Imperial Russia, dominated by the Czar, commenced using a form of the jury in 1864. At first, political crimes were not submitted to the jury, they being tried by the Czar's representatives, called Senators.

In 1871, however, eighty members of a revolutionary society were brought to trial by jury, the first public trial of political offenders in that country. What a stir this made in the citizenry! All over that vast land the details were printed, discussed, and argued over. At the conclusion of the trial, some of the eighty were found guilty, but more than three-fourths of them were found not guilty. The rejoicing in the streets was loud, but it was quite clear that the Czar wasn't so happy. He was so unhappy, in fact, that he issued a secret order depriving those found innocent of most of their privileges as a citizen, had them deported to small towns in distant parts of the Empire, and had them kept under virtual house arrest by the local officials. Furthermore, this ruler of all the Russias set up a system whereby juries selected to try political offenses had to consist of those who were hand picked by his own representatives. Thus did he avoid a repetition of being forced to bow to the people's will.

Fair stood the wind for the jury system in those years across the face of the world. There is a far different story today. Let us first look at some of the countries that still retain it and see in what manner their systems differ from that of our own country.

In England, the fountainhead of our own system, the jury procedure has been quite extensively modified and somewhat downgraded. True, the jury of twelve is still used, except in the local county courts, where juries of eight are permitted. Women are allowed to sit as jurors, although a husband and wife may not sit on the same panel. Either side, considering the nature of the case, may apply to the court to have the jury consist entirely of men or of women. In civil cases, the parties may consent to have verdicts by less than a unanimous vote. The exemptions for jurors are quite similar to our own. Members of legislatures, judges, ministers, lawyers, doctors, dentists, and members of the regular army are exempted. Citizens over sixty are likewise exempted, but are not disqualified. In the higher courts, special juries, composed of above-average citizens are sometimes used to hear important civil cases.

One of the important differences is jury selection. Unlike our own system whereby the prospective jurors may be questioned for days, the jurors in England, France, Canada, Germany, and many other countries are questioned almost exclusively by the court, or under its direction, and the whole procedure takes but a few minutes. Challenges are provided for, but these are rarely exercised. In England, in fact, usually only two questions by each attorney are permitted altogether. The first deals with whether the juror is related to the accused or the victim, and the second seeks to discover if the panelist knows of any reason why he cannot render a fair verdict based upon the evidence. Of course, the English juryman has already been selected for intelligence and character. However, it is doubtful if anyone would readily take the position that even an intelligent, high-minded individual does not have his own peculiar set of prejudices and interests.

Still, the British jury is under attack today. The requirement of unanimity to reach a verdict in a criminal case has resulted in many a "hung" jury. There has been a proposal recently to introduce majority verdicts or, at least, a less than unanimous verdict, at first glance a most democratic procedure and certain to be a time-and-effort-saver. Reasons put forward for a majority verdict in England today are that cases these days tend to be longer, more complex, and a disagreement in such a case would seriously obstruct the administration of justice if it happened very often.

The second complaint is in fact based upon the grumbling of the English police that juries are unduly favoring the criminal defendant. Leo Knowles, a British journalist, writing in the *New York Law Journal*, summarized the issue, citing the utterances of Lord Parker, the Lord Chief Justice, who pointed out that four out of every ten persons tried for serious crimes in England are acquitted. "Among the four," his Lordship added drily, "there may be an innocent man." He stated that he was aware of the fact that many people have a grudge against the police, and he felt that better results would be obtained if a majority verdict ruled and if there were a better and more careful method of selecting jurors.

The growing trend in England is to try minor crimes and offenses in magistrate's courts, without a jury. The disturbing thought comes that we are doing the very same thing in America today, because, it is said, this will help to expedite the disposition of the huge volume of such cases coming into the courts.

The grand jury, the accusatory body so important in our structure, has disappeared from England and her dominions. As a matter of fact, the grand jury we have was never a part of the general world legal system, and this includes the nations of Europe, South and Central America, Turkey, Egypt, and Japan.

Turning from Great Britain to Canada, only a relatively small number of more important criminal cases are tried before a jury. Selection of jurors follows the English pattern. There is almost no questioning and challenges are quite rare.

Two other English-based systems, those of Scotland and Ceylon, are hardly recognizable as such. In Scotland, juries have been used from the earliest times in both civil and criminal cases. The criminal jury is usually composed of fifteen members. The exemptions and challenges today are quite similar to our own system.

There are two major divergences from the Anglo-American system. First of all, majority vote rules. This seems to work out quite well in Scotland. The second distinctive feature, however, is a third alternative verdict. Not only may a jury find the defendant "guilty" or "not guilty," but it may bring in a verdict that the charge is "not proven." This means that there has been a deficiency of proof in the minds of the jury as to the guilt of the defendant, and the defendant is released. But this seems to have two major drawbacks. A jury can be divided on *three* choices, and may have a hard time reaching even a majority verdict. Also, a person who has been released because of a "not proven" verdict must carry the stigma of suspicion with him to his grave. The inference seems to be that here walks a guilty man, but one who was lucky enough to have the state unable to prove its case.

Moving on to Ceylon, what passes for a jury trial is lacking the one vital ingredient, conclusiveness. The Chief Justice may order a trial before three judges and a jury. The panel consists of seven members and at least a five-to-two verdict must be arrived at. The problem arises, however, when a jury reaches a verdict that the judges don't like. They may then ask the jury to reconsider its verdict and if it does not change its collective mind, the judges do not have to accept their verdict, but may order a new trial.

In Ireland, the grand jury was abolished in 1924 and trial by jury is used in major cases only. In civil cases, the verdict is reached when nine out of twelve jurors agree, but the verdict must be unanimous in criminal cases.

Returning to the Continent, the French system is quite different from the Anglo-American system we have discussed in detail. In fact, most of the nations of the world that did adopt the jury adopted the French system. There, juries are only used in important criminal cases. There is no finding of "guilty" or "not guilty." Instead, questions are put to the jury by the judge, much as in our own special verdicts. The judge then, on the basis of the answers to these questions, decides their legal import and reaches a decision accordingly. As to the questions, a majority vote decides the response to each.

Recently, two new elements have been added to the jury's powers in France. In the first instance, the judge will ask the jury to determine if there are any extenuating circumstances that would accrue to the benefit of the defendant. If the answer is "yes," the judge is bound to reduce the sentence. Secondly, the judge and jury deliberate together on the sentence.

In criminal trial procedure in France, three judges are present, one presiding in his capacity as President Judge. He supervises the selection of the jury, questions the defendant, and interrogates the witnesses. There are no rules of evidence. A complete story is told, irrelevancies and all. No interruption is permitted until the end of the witness' story.

Because 8 per cent of the world's criminal trials take place in the United States, we tend to think that the jury system today is world-wide. Sadly, this is not so. Outside of the United States of America, the jury system has been on the decline for a long time. It exists today in the English-speaking countries and a handful of others, such as Austria, Belgium, Denmark, Greece, Norway, and some Swiss cantons.

In many countries, it has been abolished in whole or in part. The Netherlands did away with it in 1913, Luxembourg in 1914, Portugal in 1926, Bulgaria in 1922, Egypt in 1904, Argentina in 1879, and the step has also been taken in Yugoslavia.

In Mexico, only cases involving national security or

wrongdoing by an official are tried before a jury. The panel, called a *jurado popular*, is composed of seven members whose names are chosen by lot. In all other cases, the district judge sits without a jury.

In Japan, where there is a minor case, the Summary Court may invite lay citizens, called judicial commissioners, to give opinions as to the decision to be reached in the case. But only an opinion is asked, not a verdict.

Outside of our borders, the countries that have retained jury systems are in the process of cutting down on the powers and scope of the jury. One method is to reduce the number of types of cases or crimes in which juries can be used. Civil law countries (those whose legal heritage does not stem from the common law of England) do not permit juries in civil cases, except in certain very special instances. It is held practically everywhere that juries in criminal cases are only to be used in the event of a major crime. And in many countries, those classes that would be opposed to the government are excluded from jury duty.

Another method that is changing the jury system abroad is that of having a board of lay judges regularly sit with the judge and help him reach decisions. No longer is a typical representative of the community to decide on a citizen's fate, but one who hears case after case and becomes hardened to the experience. No longer is there secret deliberation, free of interference from and not overawed by the authoritarian judicial figure in his stately robes. It is significant to note that Fascist Italy used this system in 1931, and that a similar system is used in the Soviet Union.

Why this ebbing of the jury system? It has been said that the requirements of a unanimous verdict and the extensive questioning of prospective jurors has been partly at fault, but the civil law countries that have downgraded the jury system have never had either of these two alleged defects.

Perhaps the answer to this decline of the jury system lies in the fact that in many lands, the government is afraid of the power of the people and takes every opportunity to curb such power. As an example, in Singapore, where the jury system was introduced by the British in 1826, seven years after the founding of the city, jury trials for crimes not punishable by death were abolished in 1960. Not content with this curtailing of the people's rights, the Prime Minister of Singapore, in 1969, in a power struggle to gain complete supremacy in his area, replaced seven-man juries with a panel of three state-appointed judges. He then refused all requests for access to the government-operated radio station and further refused to permit public meetings by opponents of this measure that destroyed the jury in Singapore. Perhaps the spirit of the French Revolution has died.

The fact remains that outside of the United States, only a handful of wavering countries avail themselves of the benefits of the jury system.

12 That Is the Question

THERE ARE THOSE who would do away with the jury system in America, in whole or in part. Most of these people are not unacquainted with the judicial system. Many of them are highly placed in our government and quite conversant with the administration of justice in this country today. When you find that both the former governor and the chief judge of California, the Chief Justice of the highest court of the state of New York, the chief judge of each of the states of Delaware, Massachusetts, Minnesota, Montana, and Pennsylvania, together with many well-informed scholars of jurisprudence, have advocated the abolition or curtailment of the jury system as we know it, it must be realized that there must be something wrong with the ancient Twelve, or at least a problem that must be faced and decisively answered.

What are the chief complaints of the jury critics? Basically, there are three grounds put forward.

First, it is claimed that the use of the jury in civil cases has caused excessive delay and calendar congestion in the courts, this congestion being a situation where there are thousands of cases waiting their turn for trial, while only a few jury trials at a time can be conducted. Second, critics say that the use of a jury in all cases is wasteful of the time of the courts, the participants, and the jurors, and is too costly in terms of the expense for court administration. Third, the claim is made that the quality of justice in all types of trials would be much higher if administered by a judge sitting alone.

As to excessive delay and court congestion, there is no doubt that the calendars of the courts are crowded and a person must wait seemingly forever for his day in court, especially in civil cases. Things have gotten much worse since Shakespeare's Hamlet spoke of "the law's delay."

The Institute of Judicial Administration recently conducted a survey of the courts of the land. They discovered that the average delay in reaching trial in a personal injury suit was 13.3 months for the entire nation, 22.6 months in counties having a population of more than 750,000, and 29.6 months as an average in the counties of New York state. When considering that it often takes, due to preliminary legal steps that must be taken before a case can be placed on the calendar, more than a year before the start of such a waiting period, the delay seems formidable indeed. In two counties, Cook County, Illinois, covering the city of Chicago, and in Suffolk County, a suburb of New York City, the delay runs approximately five years.

These personal injury cases constitute a great part of the civil calendar congestion. In California, where such cases make up about 50 per cent of all the cases pending, the situation has become so bad that Edmund G. Brown, when he was governor of that state, advocated an administrative bureau to handle such matters, similar in nature to the type of body that handles workmen's compensation cases in many states. It has been computed that in the Supreme Court, New York County, the average trial of an accident case, including all aspects, takes approximately four days, about two and a half times the length of a non-jury trial.

But let us look a little closer at this claim of jury-caused delay. The New York Court of Claims, dealing with cases against the state of New York, is almost two years behind on its calendar, yet does not use the jury system. Justice Walter Hart of the New York bench, while sitting in a regular trial court, has found that there is only an average three-hour difference between the jury and non-jury trial. Juries are, after all, usually selected away from the presence of the judge, while he is working on other cases, and the deliberating jury, confined to its little room, does not take up the time of the court. Openings and summations do not take up that much time and, in any event, many judges sitting alone quite often invite such remarks so they can avail themselves of the thoughts of the participating lawyers.

In a non-jury case, the judge will usually not allow himself to participate in settlement negotiations on the eve of trial in a case that he must decide, because he then technically should disqualify himself from sitting, on the grounds that he has heard allegations that may not be admissible into evidence. In jury trials, however, such taboos do not apply. He may participate in such negotiations, since it will be the jury's decision, not his. Consequently, many more jury cases than non-jury cases are settled with the aid of the court.

Note that the claim of delay and congested calendars has not been raised as to criminal cases, but only as to civil trials, and to only one type of such action, at that, the personal injury "accident" case. Is the crowded calendar due to the jury system or is it due to the fact that there are more automobiles, more accidents, and, consequently, more lawsuits?

The answer would seem to be not to abolish the jury trial in this situation, but to make modifications in the system of disposal. It must be considered whether we are willing to give up the benefits of such a democratic institution for the questionable privilege of possibly reaching trial a little sooner. It was Sir William Blackstone, the great English jurist, who said, ". . . delays and little inconveniences in the forms of justice are the price that all free nations must pay for their liberty in more substantial matters."

The second point raised by the detractors of the jury system is that it wastes time, money, and human energy. These critics cite the fact that the cost of a civil jury trial in the Supreme Court, New York County, is $3,000 per trial, representing $750 per day for the maintenance of one court room, its judge, and its court officers. Truly, time is money, and an extra day of trial is expensive. In the city of New York, it is estimated that half a million man days are devoted to jury service per year, another loss of time and money.

However, are we really spending that much in comparison with our other expenses for wars, debt reduction, schools and the like? In computing the cost of the jury system in the Federal courts, it has been found that such expenditures constitute only $\frac{1}{170}$th of 1 per cent. This is to say that you would have to pay an income tax of $17,000 for even one dollar of that sum to be considered allocated for the support of the jury system. Is this too much to pay for a bulwark of freedom and one of our most cherished institutions?

Because people lose time from their endeavors while serving as a juror, it might be supposed that they would be resentful of the burden and consider it a waste of time, something to be abolished. At least, this is what the critics of the jury claim to be the case. Let us look at three studies to see how the people feel about it.

In 1957, a questionnaire was filled out by jurors who had actually served on a panel and had completed their service. A resounding 57 per cent thought their jury experience was worthwhile; 10 per cent thought it was pleasant duty; 23 per cent found it necessary but not too pleasant. Only 9 per cent found it a waste of time and a meager 1 per cent found it downright unpleasant. Remember that these were not people talking in the abstract, but those who had actually undergone the experience.

The second survey, conducted by the University of Chicago Law School, in querying jurors who had served within a year of the time of the survey, found that 94 per cent of those responding wanted to serve again, 3 per cent were willing to do so, and only 3 per cent were against it.

On the other side of the fence, with regard to the desire to submit to a jury instead of sitting on one, the American Institute of Public Opinion, in October of 1957, released the result of a poll. The question asked of various citizens was, "Suppose you were accused of committing a not-too-serious crime. Would you rather be tried before the local judge or before a jury?" More than half, 51 per cent, to be exact, chose the jury. Only 35 per cent chose the judge, while 14 per cent did not know.

In view of these figures, is there any doubt that the jury system represents the people's choice and is quite the opposite of being "a waste of time"? As to the time "wasted" on jury duty, are the hours and days allocated to the care of our homes and our cars more important than the few short days dedicated to participation in liberty?

As a third objection, it is the critics' contention that the quality of justice would be of a much higher grade if administered by a judge alone. The judge is a man trained in the law, knowledgeable about the unreliability of men and memories, able to bring a high intelligence and experience to the weighing of the scales of justice. And who are these twelve who hold our fate in their hands? British philosopher Herbert Spencer once described a jury as "a group of twelve people of average ignorance."

If the jury was a true cross section of the community, Spencer's remark might be taken as just a witticism, but the exemptions accorded by most states withdraw from the panel those best qualified to serve—lawyers, doctors, newsmen, clergymen, and the like. In the system we use to select juries today there is no absolute guarantee that particular jurors are not unusually ignorant, secretly bigoted, credulous, just plain slow-witted, or basically narrow-minded. No tampering with the system of selection would be able to overcome this; it is inherent in our Anglo-American jury itself.

The claim has also been put forward that the jury does not follow the law as given by the judge; indeed, in most instances, though the charge to the jury by the judge may be in the simplest layman's language, the individual jurors may be incapable of understanding even that much. The belief therefore arises that the whims, prejudice, and "common sense" of the juror determine the case, thereby creating a government by man, not by laws, a condition inimical to our form of republican government. Such a situation, if true, would cause an uneven and unequal administration of justice.

Is a jury so very necessary to the determination of law-suits? The critics point to the tens of thousands of non-jury cases tried each year, without any jury advocate crying that such procedure is undemocratic. In addition, there is a branch of the law called equity, dealing with certain types of controversies in which there are no jury trials, this being an historic development of the common law. In all the centuries of such practice, there has been no hue and cry raised about the lack of a jury with regard to equity. If the jury was abolished, would this lack of complaint not also be present as to the rest of the law after a while?

The advocates of the jury system have come up with some interesting answers to the above criticisms.

As to the superiority of the trained judge over twelve amateurs, judges, too, may be overly emotional, biased, prejudiced and, considering the political system used today for most judicial selections, may even be relatively unintelligent. This failing in one man, one judge, can decide an entire case, whereas if such qualities are present in one or two jurors the effect is diluted among the twelve. As G. K. Chesterton wrote, "I would trust twelve ordinary men, but I cannot trust one ordinary man."

With regard to the memories and intelligence of jurors, most trial attorneys find that jurors do not forget facts and legal instruction quite so easily. If one forgets, another remembers. It is the collective recollection and intelligence of the twelve panelists that counts, not that of any one juror.

The heart of the question is as to whether judges would decide cases so very differently from juries. The University of Chicago Law School recently questioned some five hundred judges as to the juries over which they presided. Three thousand cases were reviewed and, in 80 per cent of them, the judges agreed with the verdicts rendered. These were trial judges, accustomed to working with juries daily. They did not speak in theory, but they based their opinions on the day-to-day workings of the courts. Of these five hundred judges, only 3 per cent thought the use of the jury should be curtailed in criminal matters and 6 per cent in civil cases.

In a further study of criminal proceedings, University of Chicago law professors Harry Kalven, Jr., and Hans

Zeisel submitted questionnaires to 550 judges across the country with reference to 3,576 jury trials over which they had presided. The results once again furnished great support for the backers of the jury system. The judges agreed with the juries 75 per cent of the time. In the other 25 per cent, the juries were primarily more lenient than the judges would have been.

It was found that juries tend to generalize from their own experience. Minor items that the law calls criminal the jurors tend to overlook, in effect saying, "There but for the grace of God go I." One-punch fights and driving after only a couple of drinks rarely find a jury ready to convict. Gambling is hardly regarded as illegal, unless it is a widespread operation.

Justice Bernard Botein, one of the leading judges of the state of New York, put the situation in perspective when he stated that in a criminal case only the jury can bring the compassion of the community into the courtroom and soften for some defendants the harshness of laws.

However, even the champions of the jury system and experts on court administration are the first to admit that there is room for improvement in the system.

One argument put forward has been the contention that the congested calendars would be cleared rapidly if there were more judges, more courtroom personnel, more facilities. Some years ago, Florida had a substantial calendar delay which was cleared up in a short time when the state constitution was amended to require automatic addition of one more judge for every fifty thousand persons added to the population of the state. Surely similar results could be obtained elsewhere with such a program.

Yes, it would cost more money. Should, however, the quality of justice be diminished by budgetary considerations, especially when the additional population will be paying taxes?

There is nothing sacrosanct about the number twelve as representing the size of a jury. Many states have provided for smaller juries, sometimes eight, often six. Justice has not noticeably suffered. Fewer jurors would have to be called, expenses would be cut, but the principle of the jury system would be maintained.

Nor are unanimous verdicts necessary. Many states only require a majority or some number less than a unanimous vote. After all, is a president elected by all the people or, as has occurred so often, by barely more than a majority? Yet, the president presides over all the people, as the less than unanimous verdict still represents the voice of the community. The purpose of such a change in the jury system is twofold. The time of deliberation would be substantially reduced and there would be fewer "hung juries."

Another suggestion made with regard to civil cases would be to have a broader and more streamlined trial procedure. Judges can urge the parties to settle their differences before trial, can narrow the issues so that the trials take a shorter time, can force sufficient disclosure of evidence in advance of trial so that a recalcitrant party will often change his position. Many states have adopted these very procedures and as a result, their calendars have shown a marked improvement. Other states could well follow these model proposals.

As will be remembered, one major criticism has been that the very people who are best qualified to sit on juries are exempted. To remedy this, Rhode Island some time ago eliminated automatic exemptions for doctors, dentists, and similar classes. Other states would do well to study the results of this change to determine if it has improved the quality of jurors.

So go the arguments for and against the jury system. There is another side to the story that must be considered.

Assume for discussion's sake that the jury today is everything its critics say it is. What of its place in our matrix of freedom and our form of government of, for, and by the people?

Sir William Blackstone, the English jurist, issued a warning to his and today's generations, when he wrote, "Every new tribunal, erected for the decision of facts, without the intervention of a jury . . . is a step towards establishing aristocracy, the most oppressive of absolute governments."

In line with this warning and in view of the experience of other nations, it is clear that the judicial bureaucracy, in the absence of a jury system, might well become subservient to governmental power, or might tend to observe the letter of the law at the expense of compassionate human values.

Too, the jury has become, in the minds of most people, a bulwark against bureaucracy, against arbitrary, biased, or corrupt actions by judges.

Justice William J. Brennan of the United States Supreme Court said only recently, "The American judiciary and bar are not justified in fostering the abolition of something which, with Americans, has been and is deeply rooted in American tradition, the right to trial by jury."

What of the proposals to abolish temporarily the jury system and "see how it works out"? Other rights of the people have been "temporarily" lost throughout the world and it is a most difficult proposition to get them restored by government which, by its very nature, seeks to retain power unto itself. What is far worse, we might grow used to the idea of the absence of the jury system, to our great loss, the loss of another important right of the people.

Sir Patrick Devlin has called the jury "the Lamp of Freedom." May that lamp never be extinguished, for if darkness prevailed, further rights would surely be lost.

As in the days of America's founding fathers, of Thomas Jefferson, of Patrick Henry, the jury remains the central pillar of the "Temple of Justice," a pillar that must remain firm so that liberty may flourish.

Appendix A: Breakdown by States as to Right to Jury

Every state, by constitution or statute, guarantees trial by jury in some form, whether in civil cases, criminal cases, or both. Most states preserve the right in both types of proceedings. In Colorado and Wyoming, however, the guarantee is specifically preserved in criminal trials, and in capital cases in Utah. Indiana and North Carolina preserve it in civil cases.

While every state has jury trials in some form, there are variations, some of which are as follows:

ALABAMA: The legislature may authorize trials for misdemeanors without a jury.

ALASKA: The right to trial by jury is preserved if the amount in controversy is at least $250. In civil actions, the legislature may provide for verdict by ¾ vote. In courts not of record, the legislature may provide for juries of from six to twelve members.

ARIZONA: In courts not of record, the legislature may provide for juries of less than twelve members. In civil actions in courts of record, where the parties consent, the verdict may be reached by nine or more jurors. The legislature may provide for waiver in civil cases if the parties agree.

ARKANSAS: In civil cases, a verdict may be reached by nine or more jurors. Waiver may be had in all cases as prescribed by law.

CALIFORNIA: In both civil actions and misdemeanors, the parties may agree on a verdict by any number less than twelve. In civil actions, the jury may reach a verdict by a $\frac{3}{4}$ vote. Civil juries may be waived. Criminal juries may also be waived, if agreed to by prosecutor, defendant, and defendant's attorney.

COLORADO: In all civil cases and in criminal cases in courts not of record, the number of jurors may be less than twelve, as prescribed by law.

CONNECTICUT: Agreement may be made in civil cases on a verdict of nine of twelve jurors.

DELAWARE: In certain counties, an indictment may be voted by a grand jury if nine of fifteen agree; in other counties, seven of ten.

FLORIDA: The legislature may reduce the number of jurors in any court to not less than six.

GEORGIA: In other than the Superior Court, the legislature may reduce the number of jurors to not less than five.

HAWAII: The right to a jury is preserved if the amount in suit is in excess of one hundred dollars. Verdicts may be by $\frac{3}{4}$ vote, if the legislature so provides.

IDAHO: A $\frac{3}{4}$ vote is necessary in civil cases. The legislature may provide for $\frac{5}{6}$ vote in misdemeanors. In both civil actions and misdemeanors, the parties may agree to any number of jurors less than twelve. The jury may be waived in all cases not amounting to a felony.

ILLINOIS: The legislature has the power to provide for a lesser number than twelve jurors in civil actions.

INDIANA: The jury may determine the facts and the law in all criminal cases.

IOWA: In inferior courts, the legislature may provide for less than twelve jurors.

KANSAS: The right to trial by jury may be waived.

KENTUCKY: In civil cases, and in misdemeanors in courts below the Circuit Court, a jury of six is provided for. In Circuit Court, the legislature may provide for $\frac{3}{4}$ vote in civil cases.

LOUISIANA: Where hard labor may not be assessed as a punishment, trial is by judge alone. Where sentence may be at hard labor, a jury of five must reach a unanimous verdict. Where the punishment is necessarily at hard labor, nine jurors out of twelve must concur. Where capital punishment is provided for, a unanimous verdict by a jury of twelve is required.

MAINE: A criminal trial must be in the vicinity of the crime, except for trials by martial law or impeachment.

MARYLAND: In criminal cases, the jury shall be the judges of both the facts and the law. Waiver is available in all cases.

MASSACHUSETTS: The legislature has the right to abolish the jury with respect to cases arising on the high seas or with regard to mariners' wages.

MICHIGAN: Where a jury of twelve is provided in civil actions, ten must concur for a verdict. In criminal cases in courts not of record, the jury may be less than twelve. In civil cases, the jury is waived unless demanded in conformity with law.

MINNESOTA: The legislature may provide that after six hours of deliberation in civil cases, a verdict may be arrived at by a 5⁄6 vote. Waiver may be had in all cases, as prescribed by law.

MISSISSIPPI: In civil actions in Circuit and Chancery Courts, the legislature may provide for a verdict of nine out of twelve.

MISSOURI: In courts not of record, the legislature may provide in both civil and criminal cases for less than twelve jurors. In civil cases in these courts, the legislature may provide for a 2⁄3 vote. In courts of record, however, there must be a 3⁄4 vote in civil actions. In criminal cases, the defendant may waive trial by jury if the court consents.

MONTANA: A jury of six is provided for in civil cases and in misdemeanors in Justice Court. In civil actions and criminal trials for less than felonies, verdict may consist of 2⁄3 vote. In both civil and criminal cases, the jury may be waived.

NEBRASKA: In courts inferior to the District Court, the legislature may provide for less than twelve jurors, and may provide for 5⁄6 vote in civil cases.

NEVADA: In civil trials, verdict may be by 3⁄4 vote, except that the legislature has the right to change this to a requirement of a unanimous vote. The jury may be waived in civil cases.

NEW HAMPSHIRE: There is a right to a jury trial if the amount in contention is over five hundred dollars.

NEW JERSEY: The legislature may provide for a 5⁄6 vote in civil suits and in cases not involving more than fifty dollars, a jury of six.

NEW MEXICO: The legislature may provide for a less than unanimous vote in civil cases. In courts inferior to the district court, the jury may consist of six members.

NEW YORK: In civil actions, there may be a ⅚ vote. In both civil cases and criminal cases not involving capital punishment, the jury may be waived.

NORTH CAROLINA: In petty misdemeanors, the legislature may provide for other means of trial, besides that of a jury trial. Juries may be waived in all cases, in which event the findings of fact by the judge have the validity of a verdict.

NORTH DAKOTA: In civil actions in courts not of record, the legislature may provide for a jury of less than twelve.

OHIO: The legislature may provide a ¾ vote in civil actions.

OKLAHOMA: In courts of record other than the County Court, the jury is composed of twelve. In County Court and courts not of record, six. A ¾ vote is provided for in civil actions and for crimes less than felonies.

OREGON: Except for first-degree murder, ten out of twelve is sufficient for a verdict in criminal trials in Circuit Court. A ¾ vote in civil cases constitutes a verdict. In all criminal cases, with the exception of capital offenses, the jury may be waived in writing, with the consent of the trial judge.

PENNSYLVANIA: Standard trial procedure. Jury may be waived in civil cases and in criminal cases, too, except for murder and treason.

RHODE ISLAND: Standard trial procedure. May have both special and general verdicts at the same time in civil cases.

SOUTH CAROLINA: In both civil and criminal jury cases in Municipal Court and courts inferior to Circuit Courts a jury of six is provided for.

SOUTH DAKOTA: The legislature may provide that the jury shall be less than twelve in courts not of record, and for a ¾ vote in civil cases.

TENNESSEE: Standard trial procedure.

TEXAS: In civil actions and for crimes less than a felony, nine may constitute a verdict in District Court. In County Court, the jury shall be six. In all cases, entitled to jury if application made in open court and fee paid, or affidavit filed that fee cannot be paid.

UTAH: Except for capital cases, juries shall consist of eight in courts of general jurisdiction. They may consist of four in courts of inferior jurisdiction. Unanimous verdicts are required in criminal trials, while a ¾ vote is required in civil actions. In civil cases, the jury is waived, unless demanded.

VERMONT: Standard trial procedure. The jury may be waived in civil cases and in criminal cases where the offense is not punishable by death or imprisonment in state prison.

VIRGINIA: In civil actions in courts not of record, the legislature may limit the number of jurors to five in cases cognizable by Justice of Peace, or seven in other cases. In offenses less than felonies, the law may provide for juries of less than twelve, but not less than five. The jury may be waived.

WASHINGTON: In civil actions in courts of record, a verdict may be reached by nine or more. In courts not of record, the legislature may provide for less than twelve jurors. The legislature may provide for waiver in civil cases, where the parties agree.

WEST VIRGINIA: In civil trials before a justice, the jury may be six. A jury in civil cases is waived unless demanded.

WISCONSIN: In civil actions, the legislature may provide for at least a ⅚ vote. Waiver may be made in all cases, as prescribed by law.

WYOMING: The legislature may provide for juries of less than twelve in all civil trials in all courts, and in criminal cases in courts not of record.

Appendix B: Means of Indoctrinating Juries Today

Many of the states use various methods to educate jurors, including speeches of welcome and instruction when the prospective jurors are first assembled. Some jurisdictions exhibit motion pictures to the jurymen showing the workings of the jury system. One picture is called "The True and the Just," and was produced with the help of a Ford Foundation grant. Its purpose was to answer the complaints of previous jurors as to the mechanics of the system, such as waiting around to be called, the frequency of being summoned for service and, after selection of a jury, the letdown when the case is settled on the eve of trial. A half-hour documentary, it has already been shown to some 300,000 people in New York City and approximately one and a half million across the country. Justice Bernard Botein of the Appellate Division in New York says that since the showing of the film to prospective jurors was instituted, the huge number of grumbling letters he used to receive from irate ex-jurors has dwindled to zero.

144

Another and more popular means of informing panelists of their responsibilities is the dissemination of jurors' handbooks, covering in general the entire procedure of a trial and the jury's place in it. Many states have done this, as well as the Federal courts. As a typical example, the following is reprinted from the handbook of information for jurors serving in the courts of two of New York City's five boroughs, the counties of New York and the Bronx.

A HANDBOOK OF INFORMATION
FOR TRIAL

JURORS

Serving in the Courts
of the
Counties of New York and the Bronx

INTRODUCTION

You have been chosen to serve as a juror in the Courts of New York. Your selection has been made under the laws of our State which are designed to distribute this responsibility equally among all persons qualified for jury service.

This booklet has been prepared to assist you in discharging your duties in an efficient and intelligent manner. You are urged to study it carefully.

IMPORTANCE OF JURY SERVICE

Trial by jury is one of the cornerstones of judicial administration. Under our American system of administering justice the persons who compose the jury are a part of the Court itself. Your work, therefore, is as important as the work of the judge who presides at the trial. Because of this importance, jury service is one of the highest duties of citizenship.

The cases which require your services involve disputes of fact. Your duty as a juror is to consider carefully the evidence presented in the case and to determine the true facts. To these facts you must then apply the law as defined to you by the judge.

Sound judgment, absolute integrity and complete impartiality are expected of you as a juror. Remember that each case in which you sit is a matter of grave importance to the parties involved. If you are to fulfill your obligation as a juror under the oath which you will take, you should render the same thoughtful consideration and attention that you would expect from a jury in a case in which you were a party.

LITIGANTS AND PLEADINGS

The party who commences the lawsuit is called the plaintiff. In criminal cases the State of New York is always the plaintiff. The party against whom the action is brought is called the defendant. A party may be an individual or may be a firm or corporation.

The plaintiff's claim is asserted in a complaint. The defendant gives his defense in an answer. Sometimes a defendant asserts a claim against the plaintiff. This is called a counter claim. These papers are called pleadings. Thus, each party has a right to be informed of his adversary's claim against him.

It is in this general way that the issues are clearly defined for presentation to the court, and to you, as jurors, for a verdict, based on your search for the truth.

•

PROCEDURE IN CIVIL CASES

The trial begins with the selection of the jurors. In order that a completely impartial jury may be selected, prospective jurors will be questioned either by the judge or by the attorneys. You should answer their questions frankly and accurately, bearing in mind that their purpose is to determine whether any prospective juror should be excused from participating in the case. The law also permits the attorney for each party to "challenge" a certain number of jurors without assigning any specific reason for doing so. If you are so "challenged," you should not feel that this is done on any personal basis nor to secure any unfair advantage to any party. It involves no reflection whatever upon the juror so excused.

After you have been selected to participate in a particular case as a juror, you are required to take a solemn oath that you will "well and truly try the issues and render a true verdict according to the evidence."

The examination and selection of jurors in civil cases is often conducted by counsel outside the court room, either in the jurors' assembly room or in an adjoining room. This is done to conserve the judge's time so that he may proceed with other judicial business while your jury is being impanelled, but he always maintains supervision over the impanelling of the panel.

Ordinarily the jury is composed of 12 persons. However, the parties have the option of proceeding with a jury of 6 persons. Where a trial is likely to be protracted, "alternate," or additional, jurors may be selected, so that a substitute will be available should one of the regular jurors become ill during the course of the trial.

Upon the opening of the case, the attorney for the plaintiff presents to the judge and the jury a statement of the facts upon which the plaintiff intends to rely in order to succeed. The attorney for the defendant then states his client's position in opposition. The opening statements by the lawyers for the respective parties are not evidence. They are merely outlines of what each side hopes to prove. Their purpose is to enable you to follow the evidence more easily.

The evidence, oral or documentary, is then presented for the jury's consideration by the respective attorneys under the supervision of the judge. After all of the evidence has been received, arguments are made by the attorneys of both parties.

The judge will then deliver his instructions, commonly referred to as a "charge," to the jury. The purpose of the "charge" is to inform the jury of the law which must be applied to the various factual determinations which the jury may reach.

After the judge has delivered his "charge" the jurors retire to a place of privacy for their deliberations. It is the duty of the foreman of the jury to see that the deliberations are carried on in an orderly fashion. In reaching its verdict the jury should first determine the truth of the factual matters in dispute and then apply the proper law as "charged" by the judge. When the jury reaches its decision it returns to the courtroom and announces its verdict through the jury foreman to the judge.

The verdict in a civil case requires the agreement of at least five-sixths of the jurors; ten jurors when the jury is composed of twelve persons, and five jurors when the jury is composed of six persons.

•

PROCEDURE IN CRIMINAL CASES

The laws of this state require that the defendant in a criminal case be indicted by a Grand Jury or be named in an information filed by the District Attorney or other prosecutor before he can be made to stand trial.

An indictment is a written complaint voted by a majority of the members of the Grand Jury after having heard only evidence presented by the District Attorney. Neither an indictment nor an information is evidence in the case or proof of guilt. It is merely the legal means by which the defendant is brought before the court. It is the evidence at the trial which alone may be considered by the jury.

In all cases with which you, as a juror, are concerned, the defendant has answered the charge of the indictment or information by pleading "Not Guilty."

The procedure in criminal cases is similar to that in civil cases. Differences will be revealed to you in the course of the trial through your own observations and the instructions of the judge.

The jury's verdict in a criminal case is required to be unanimous.

•

PROCEDURE IN SURROGATE'S COURT

Jurors who are to serve in the Surrogate's Court are selected from the panel of jurors in attendance at the Supreme Court.

The jurisdiction of the Surrogate's Court pertains particularly to the estates of deceased persons. There are two types of proceedings in which juries commonly act. One is a proceeding in which the validity of a last will and testament of a deceased person is attacked, and this is known as a contested probate proceeding. The issues in such a contest ordinarily pertain to the proper signing, witnessing, and publishing of the will, the mental capacity of the decedent, and whether decedent was subjected to any improper influence or fraud.

The second type of proceeding is known as a discovery proceeding, in which the executor or the administrator, acting as the representative of a decedent's estate, endeavors to recover personal property or money which he contends belongs to the decedent's estate, while the person against whom the proceeding is brought claims the ownership of the personal property or money in dispute.

In all jury cases in the Surrogate's Court, particular questions are submitted to the jury for answer and the surrogate charges the jurors as to the applicable law with regard to the questions submitted to them.

As in other civil cases, a verdict in the Surrogate's Court requires the concurrence of ten of the twelve jurors.

•

JUROR'S CONDUCT

It is of the utmost importance that you faithfully obey the following rules of conduct during your period of service as a juror:

1. Be punctual in the performance of your duties.
2. Give undivided attention to the evidence and the proceedings of the trial.
3. Do not discuss the cases, evidence or trial proceedings with anyone nor permit another to engage you in conversation in these matters. If there is an attempt to engage you in such discussion, whether innocently or corruptly, ascertain the name of the person involved and report the incident immediately to the judge.
4. Since the attorneys you may meet in the court house or its vicinity may participate in a case in which you are called upon to serve a juror, you should not enter into conversation with them during your term of service as a juror.
5. Do not discuss the evidence or the trial proceedings with your fellow jurors prior to deliberation in the jury room at the close of the case. Any views formed before the judge's charge are premature and any comments made to fellow jurors during the course of the trial may be misconstrued or may embarrass you in expressing yourself in the jury room after hearing all the evidence and the judge's charge.
6. Do not undertake a personal investigation of a case in which you are serving as a juror, either by visiting the scene of the occurrence or by talking with the parties, their attorneys or witnesses. Your decision should result from what happens in the courtroom and nowhere else. If the judge considers that it is necessary for you to visit the scene, he will make arrangements for all members of the jury to do so under his direction.
7. Your verdicts must be impartial and free from passion, prejudice, sympathy or any unjust influence. You are to apply the law as stated by the judge and no one else.

8. Be faithful to the high trust committed to you, remembering the full measure of your responsibilities and the solemnity of the oath administered to you at each trial in which you serve. As members of the jury, you are entitled at any time, even after retirement for deliberations, to request instructions from the judge concerning your duties.

•

CO-OPERATION

Complete co-operation between Court and jury is essential to proper judicial administration. The Court is aware that your service as a juror requires a temporary absence from your usual vocation. It will extend every reasonable consideration for your comfort and convenience and will seek to conserve the time of the jurors to the utmost. Occasions will arise when your services are not required, and the Court may temporarily excuse you so that you may attend to your private affairs.

Do not become impatient if you are conpelled to wait before service as a juror in a case. It is not the fault of the clerk who has you in charge. It is not due to a lack of consideration of your time by the court. There is no way of ascertaining how long it will take to dispose of cases ahead. Unless there are a sufficient number of jurors in reserve, the court would be unable to function. The fact that you are available constitutes an important part of your service.

If sudden illness or other emergency prevents your appearance at Court, notify the jury clerk as soon as possible. (In New York County—DIgby 9-2600, Extensions 295, 297 and 298; in Bronx County—CYpress 3-8000, Extensions 232 and 233.)

If, after your service as a juror, you have any suggestions for improving jury service, please send your suggestions to: Department Director of Administration, Appellate Division, First Department, 27 Madison Avenue, New York, N.Y. 10010. The court invites your thoughtful comments.

•

GENERAL INFORMATION

1. You will ordinarily receive at least ten days notice when called for service as a juror.

2. A person who has been notified to attend as a juror and who desires to be excused should personally present the jury summons to the Court. Personal appearance will be excused only upon presentation of written proof of absence from the city or physical disability which prevents the juror's appearance. The jury summons should be submitted with such an application. Proof of physical disability shall be in the form of a physician's certificate, which shall state the nature of the illness and when the juror is expected to recover. A juror who is absent from the city at the time the jury summons is served, and who will not return until after the date service is to begin, must provide written proof of the same.

   The dates and times when requests to be excused may be presented are noted upon the jury summons.

3. Wilful disobedience of a jury summons is a criminal contempt of court and is punishable by a fine of $250 or imprisonment for not exceeding 30 days, or both.

4. Each person summoned to serve as a trial juror, unless excused by the Court, must be available for service for at least ten working days. It is possible that a trial may extend beyond that period.

5. A fee of $12.00 for each day's necessary attendance in Court will be mailed to the juror by the Department of Finance, Municipal Building, New York City (Phone 566-2571), where all inquiries regarding payment should be addressed.

6. Desks, pen, ink and telephones are available in the jury assembly rooms, so that, in case of unexpected delay, jurors may transact their personal affairs while awaiting selection for service in a particular case. Smoking, reading of books and magazines, and brief consultations with office associates and employees are not out of order. But purely social visits are not permitted.

7. Jurors may not serve more often than once in two years.

8. Jurors who change their names, residences or business addresses, should promptly notify the County Clerk of the County in which they reside (County Clerk, New York County, 60 Centre Street, New York, N.Y. 10007; County

Clerk, Bronx County, 851 Grand Concourse, Bronx, N.Y. 10451).

•

CONCLUSION

Your reward in serving as a juror lies in the fact that you have performed a high duty of citizenship by aiding in the maintenance of law and order and in the administration of justice among your fellow men. It is hoped that your contribution to this important function of government will be an enlightening and interesting experience and that at the conclusion of your service you will enjoy the satisfaction of having performed an important duty.

Appendix C: Specifics of New York State Jury Law

Although covered in general in Chapter V, the various sections of New York state law dealing with the jury are lengthy and labyrinthine and should be carefully read if one is to fully understand the mechanics of the jury procedure as set up by the New York state legislature, which is somewhat similar to most other states' procedures. Most sections dealing with the jury are to be found in the Judiciary Law of the State of New York. Not all such sections are germane to an understanding of the field, so the following constitutes a carefully selected grouping of those provisions most vital to the jury process.

§ 652. County jury board

There shall be established for each county, a county jury board which, except in the counties of Albany, Westchester, Suffolk and Nassau, shall consist of the justice of the supreme court, who may be a justice of the appellate division, resident in the county, or, if there is more than one such justice resident in the county, the justices of the appellate division of the department embracing the county shall designate one of them, or, if there be none resident in the county, the justices of the appellate division of the department embracing the county shall designate one, resident in the district embracing the county; the county judge, or if there be more than one, the senior county judge, except that in a county where a county judge may engage in the private practice of law, another justice of the supreme court from the judicial district, who may be a justice of the appellate division, shall be designated as a member of the county board in the place of the county judge, by the justices of the appellate division; and any member of the county board of supervisors who shall be designated for that purpose by the board of supervisors but no supervisor shall be designated if he engages in the practice of law. Designation of a justice of the supreme court and of the supervisor shall be in writing, filed in the office of the clerk of the county, and shall continue in effect until changed.

In the county of Albany the county jury board shall consist of the county judge, the surrogate and a member of the board of supervisors to be designated as set forth above. In the county of Westchester the county jury board shall consist of the senior county judge, the surrogate and the chairman of the county board. In the counties of Nassau and Suffolk the county jury board shall consist of the justices of the supreme court residing in the county, the surrogate and the county judges.

The county jury board shall exercise the powers and duties in regard to the commissioner and in regard to the selection of grand jurors as prescribed by this article.

The commissioner shall consult with the county jury board in regard to the proper and efficient administration of the jury system, and shall act as secretary to the board.

§ 657. Specific powers and duties of commissioner

The commissioner shall be an officer of all courts of record located in the county in which he acts and shall have authority to administer oaths or affirmations as to any matter relating to his duties under this article or the rules adopted pursuant thereto.

He shall keep a record of all proceedings before him, or in his office.

He shall furnish a copy of each paper filed or proceeding taken in his office, to any person applying therefor and paying the fees, except that answers, data and information obtained in interviewing and examining prospective jurors shall be considered confidential and shall not be disclosed except to the county jury board or as permitted by the appellate divisions. The commissioner shall charge the same fees for furnishing copies of papers as the clerk of a court of record and shall pay over all such fees to the county treasurer.

The commissioner may designate from among the members of his staff, by a certificate filed in his office, any deputy or assistant to perform any of his duties as required by law.

Whenever reference is made to the commissioner in this article or the rules adopted pursuant thereto, such reference shall be deemed to apply also to deputies or assistants duly designated by him, except where the contrary intent is plainly apparent from the context.

In accordance with the law and the rules adopted pursuant thereto, each commissioner shall

(1) determine the competence, qualifications, eligibility and liability of individuals for jury service, and make inquiries and conduct examinations of persons as to themselves, and if necessary as to others, anywhere within the county and shall have power to issue and enforce notices, mandates and summonses,

(2) hear and determine claims for exemption from jury service,

(3) prepare ballots for all qualified jurors for use in the supreme court, county court, surrogate's court and district court,

(4) furnish to each city or town clerk on or before the thirty-first day of December, or such other date as may be prescribed by rule of the justices of the appellate division for the use pursuant to section two hundred and twenty of the justice court act; of all inferior courts within the city or town during the ensuing twelve months, a list of the names of qualified jurors resident in the city or town, a sealed box, or other device containing ballots of the names of the qualified trial jurors resident in the city or town, together with a list, alphabetically arranged of the names in the box so furnished, or

(5) furnish to each clerk, and where there is no clerk, to the justice of any court not of record, or any city or municipal court of record, on or before the thirty-first day of December, or such other date as may be prescribed by rule of the justices of the appellate division for the use of all these inferior courts during the ensuing twelve months, a list of names of qualified jurors resident in the city or town, a sealed

box or other device containing ballots of the names of the qualified trial jurors resident in the city or town, together with a list alphabetically arranged of the names in the box or other device so furnished.

(6) draw panels of grand and trial jurors for all terms of the supreme court, county court, surrogate's court and the district court,

(7) notify and summon jurors drawn for service in those courts for which he has drawn them, or direct the sheriff to notify or summon such jurors,

(8) take any steps necessary to bring about the punishment of those who violate the laws and rules relating to the selection, drawing, summoning and empaneling of jurors,

(9) consult with the county jury board as provided in section six hundred fifty-two, and

(10) do all things necessary and proper for the true execution of his powers and duties.

No part of this section shall operate to impair the right to challenge a particular juror at a trial.

§ 658. Source of names

The commissioner, in order to ascertain names of persons eligible as jurors, may consult the latest census enumeration, the latest published city, town or village telephone or other directory, the assessment rolls, the voters' registry list and any other general source of names. There shall be continuous search for persons qualified and liable for jury service, in order to obtain as many prospective jurors as necessary and in order to limit as much as possible repetition of jury service.

Each public officer of the county and of every city, town or village within the county, shall, upon written request, at all times furnish to the commissioner, without charge, all the information within his control to enable the commissioner to procure the names of persons who may be eligible to serve as jurors, as well as information concerning a person's qualifications or lack of qualifications for jury service.

§ 659. Examination as to fitness

No person's name shall be entered on a jury ballot or list unless he has stated to the commissioner, in a certificate or questionnaire pursuant to section 210.45 of the penal law, his qualifications in writing in his own hand and has signed such certificate or questionnaire.

In order to ascertain a juror's qualifications, the commissioner may either

(1) mail to the prospective juror a questionnaire form on which to enter the name, address, occupation, claims for exemption and such other questions as the law may require, which the person to whom the questionnaire is mailed must fill out in his own hand, sign and return within one week to the commissioner; or

(2) summon the prospective juror to appear before him for the purpose of filling out the questionnaire and testifying as to the competence, qualifications, eligibility and liability of himself or any other person to serve as a juror and to present claims for exemption or disqualification. Such person shall not be entitled to any fee or mileage when responding for such purpose. Such summons may be served personally or by leaving it at the person's residence or place of business with a person of suitable age and discretion, or by mail. If served personally or by substitution the summons shall require the person summoned to attend not less than three days after service. If served by mail the summons shall require the person summoned to attend not less than five days after the mailing thereof.

One or more successive summonses may be served upon the same person when he fails to attend as required by a former summons. When a person has so attended twice and furnished all information required, he shall not be required to attend again for one year thereafter.

The commissioner may, in his discretion, dispense with examination of the person so notified where another person cognizant of the facts is produced and testifies in his stead and it appears from the testimony of such other person that the person notified is disqualified, not qualified or exempt.

The commissioner may, in his discretion, forward to any appropriate police authorities within the county for checking against the records of such authorities, the names of any or all persons found otherwise qualified by him for jury service.

Notwithstanding the foregoing provisions of this section, the justices of the appellate division may by rule require that, in any county contained within their respective departments,

(a) the questionnaires required in accordance with option numbered (1) above shall be filled out in the prospective juror's own hand, signed and returned to the commissioner,

(b) each prospective juror shall be personally examined by the commissioner,

(c) the names of prospective jurors found otherwise qualified shall be forwarded by the commissioner to the appropriate police authorities within the county for checking against the records of such authorities.

§ 660. Questionnaires; index cards

Each questionnaire, filled out as required by section six hundred fifty-nine, shall be contained on a card or other paper of a size convenient for handling and shall be substantially as set forth in section six hundred sixty-one unless otherwise prescribed by rule of the justices of the appellate division.

In addition to the questionnaire there shall be made out for each person called upon to qualify as a juror, an index card containing the name of said person, whether he has qualified for jury service or whether he is disqualified, has been rejected, or is otherwise not eligible or liable for service, whether he has been chosen for the grand jury, and such other information as may be deemed desirable by the commissioner and which may be conveniently inserted on the card. These cards shall be filed alphabetically according to the last name of the person, regardless of whether or not he is eligible or liable for jury service. They shall be keyed to the questionnaires and shall constitute an index of all persons called upon to qualify as jurors. They shall be kept, if possible, in a visible index file.

A commissioner, instead of using index cards, may keep the required information in properly indexed books. In such event, whenever index cards are referred to, the reference shall be deemed to include such books.

Upon the basis of the questionnaire and examination, if any, the commissioner shall decide whether the person is qualified to serve as a juror. In accordance with the decision he shall note on each questionnaire, in a prominent place, whether the person has been accepted, or found disqualified, not qualified or granted exemption; if accepted, the jury for which he has been chosen shall be noted; if disqualified, not qualified or granted exemption, the reason shall be noted. Where jurors are not qualified, the reason therefor may be indicated by appropriate language or by the symbols R1, R2, R3, R4, R5 and R6 representing the six subdivisions of section six hundred sixty-two. Likewise, exemptions may be indicated by appropriate language or by the symbols E1, E2, E3, E4, E5, E6, E7 and E8 representing the eight subdivisions of section six hundred sixty-five, and disqualifications may be indicated by appropriate language or by the symbols D1, D2, D3, D4, D5 and D6 representing the six subdivisions of section six hundred sixty-four.

Before examining persons, the commissioner shall check their names against the index cards of names of persons previously examined.

The questionnaires of persons accepted and the questionnaires of persons rejected shall be filed separately, each in alphabetical order. Whenever any person qualified for jury service becomes exempt or disqualified for reasons accruing since his examination, his questionnaire shall be marked accordingly and transferred to an inactive file. The index card of such person shall also be marked accordingly.

The questionnaires of persons rejected, or who died or who have become unqualified or exempt for reasons accruing since their examination, shall be kept in the inactive file at least for one year thereafter.

In counties employing electronic means for drawing the names of qualified trial jurors, correct changes shall be made in the code input, magnetic tape, perforated paper tape and cards, or microfilm to add the names of persons who become qualified or to delete the names of those who become disqualified for jury service in accordance with the provisions of this article.

§ 661. Form of questionnaire

The questionnaire to be filled out by prospective jurors shall contain the substantially following information and shall be in such form as the commissioner may prescribe.

QUALIFICATIONS TO SERVE AS JUROR
TO BE FILLED OUT IN OWN HANDWRITING

The undersigned certifies to the following answers (EXPLANATIONS OR REMARKS CONCERNING ANSWERS) *
MAY BE MADE IN RULED BOX ON REVERSE SIDE) *

A PERSON WHO KNOWINGLY MAKES A FALSE STATEMENT OF A MATERIAL FACT IN
THIS QUESTIONNAIRE IS GUILTY OF A MISDEMEANOR, PUNISHABLE BY FINE AND IMPRISONMENT

1. Print name in full_____
   First Name　　　　　Middle Name　　　　Last Name
   Married___Single___Widower__No. of
   Divorced___Separated____Children

2. Date of
   birth_____ Color
   Mo.　Day　Year　hair_____ Color
   eyes_____ Wear
   glasses_____ Height_____
   Weight_____

3. Residence_____ Zip Code_____
   Apt.
   No.____ Tel.
   No.____

4. Are you　　If not, with
   the tenant____whom do you live_____ How long living
   at present address_____ How long in
   N. Y. State_____ In N. Y.
   County____

5. Former residences
   for past six years_____

6. Give any other name you
   have used or been known by_____ Did you register
   at last election_____ Where did you
   live then_____

7. Place of
   Birth_____ If not American born,
   City　　　State　how became citizen_____ When
   naturalized_____ Where_____

8. Education: Primary, High School,
   College, degrees, special studies, etc._____

9. Occupation_____ Employed
   at present_____ Business
   address_____ Zip Code____ Tel.
   No._____

10. Firm name
    of employer _____ How long in
    present employment_____

11. What other employment
    during past six years_____

12. Wife's
    name_____ Her
    occupation_____ Her
    firm_____ Her busi-
    ness address____

13. Ever before filled out
    this or similar form_____ Ever served
    as a juror_____ In what court and
    when did you last serve___

14. Ever been denied listing as a qualified juror
    or been stricken from any list of jurors____ Where
    and why___

15. Are you physically
    disabled or incapacitated____ Is your hearing or eyesight so impaired that
    you could not intelligently follow a case in court___ Ever confined to a State
    or Private Institution___

16. Ever arrested
    or indicted on a　　Ever
    criminal charge____convicted__ Ever summoned or notified to
    answer charges before any admin-
    istrative Bureau or Public Officer___ Any judgment ever entered against
    you in a civil court on allegations
    of fraud or misconduct___

17. If your answer to any question on lines
    15 or 16 is "Yes", give all particulars___

18. Any judgments　Nature of
    outstanding　　action in
    against　　　　which
    you_____obtained___ Are you knowingly a member of any party or organization which advocates, advises or
    teaches the duty, necessity, desirability, or propriety of overthrowing or destroying the
    government of the United States, the government of any state, territory, district or
    possession thereof, or of any political subdivision therein, by force or violence?___

19. Have you ever been in
    bankruptcy or made a general
    assignment for the benefit of creditors___ Have you such views concerning the death penalty
    as would prevent you from finding a defendant
    guilty if the crime charged be punishable by death__

20. Have you any opinion as to circumstantial
    evidence which would prevent your finding
    a verdict of guilty upon such evidence___ Do you doubt your ability to lay aside an opinion or impression formed
    from newspaper reading or otherwise, or to render an impartial verdict
    upon the evidence, uninfluenced by any such opinion or impression___

21. Are you aware of any prejudice against any
    state law which would prevent a finding of
    guilt for violating such law___ Have you such a prejudice against any particular
    defense to a criminal charge as would prevent your
    finding a fair and impartial verdict upon its merits__

22. By law the failure of a defendant in a criminal case to
    testify is not considered as any evidence of his guilt.
    Would you give a defendant the benefit of this law___ Is there anything which would influence you as a juror,
    as affecting any person, or class of persons because of
    nationality, sex, color, race, religion, wealth, occupation,
    political affiliation, social or economic belief or any other
    reason___

Examiner's recommendation_____

THE FOREGOING ANSWERS ARE TRUE IN ALL RESPECTS

THE MAKING OF A FALSE STATEMENT OF A MATERIAL
FACT IN THIS QUESTIONNAIRE IS A MISDEMEANOR,
PUNISHABLE BY FINE AND IMPRISONMENT.

SIGN HERE_____

_____do hereby certify;

I do not dwell or lodge nor do I have or maintain a dwelling or lodging in the County of New York for the greater part of the time between the first day of October and the thirtieth day of June next thereafter, and I am not a resident

of said County; but I reside permanently at_____

City of_____, County of_____, State of_____, and have

resided there since_____.

person who knowingly
makes a false statement of a
material fact in this certificate is guilty of a Class A
misdemeanor, punishable by
fine and imprisonment. (Penal
Law, Sec. 210.45.) _____
                                    Signature

Dated:_____197___ _____
                                    EXAMINER

_____do hereby certify;

I am entitled to and claim exemption } from doing jury service for the following
I am disqualified   }

reason _____

person who knowingly
makes a false statement of a
material fact in this certificate is guilty of a Class A
misdemeanor, punishable by
fine and imprisonment. (Penal
Law, Sec. 210.45.) _____
                                    Signature

Dated:_____197___ _____
                                    EXAMINER

| NAME | ADDRESS | BIRTH DATE | INDEX NO. |

RECORD OF JURY SERVICE

DATE PLACED IN WHEEL	TERM DRAWN	COURT	DAYS IN ATTEND-ANCE	DAYS ACTUAL-LY SERVED	IF EXCUSED REASON	DATE PLACED IN WHEEL	TERM DRAWN	COURT	DAYS IN ATTEND-ANCE	DAYS ACTUAL-LY SERVED	IF EXCUSED REASON

CHANGE OF ADDRESS

BUSINESS ADDRESS

RESIDENCE

§ 662. Qualifications of jurors

In order to be qualified to serve as a juror a person must:

1. Be a citizen of the United States, and a resident of the county.

2. Be not less than twenty-one, nor more than seventy-two years of age, provided however, that a person between seventy and seventy-two years of age shall be excused at the request of any party to the action and such request shall not constitute a peremptory challenge.

3. Be in the possession of his natural faculties and not infirm or decrepit.

4. Not have been convicted of a felony or of a misdemeanor involving moral turpitude.

5. Be of sound mind and good character; of approved integrity; of sound judgment; and able to read and write the English language understandably.

A person dwelling or lodging or having or maintaining a dwelling or lodging in a county for the greater part of the time between October first and June thirtieth next thereafter, or a resident therein more than six months of the year, is a resident of that county, within the meaning of this section.

§ 663. Jurors with scruples against death penalty

No person shall be selected to serve as a grand juror or as a trial juror in a criminal action, the punishment for which is or may be the infliction of the death penalty, who has stated in his statement to the commissioner that he has conscientious scruples against the death penalty which would prevent him from finding a verdict of guilty of any crime punishable by death.

§ 664. Disqualifications

Each of the following officers is disqualified to serve as a juror:

1. Any duly elected federal, state, city, county, town or village official;

2. The comptroller; the attorney-general; the head of a civil department or the head and members of a board, council or commission which is the head of a civil department of the federal, state, city, county, town or village government; members of the state tax

commission; members of the state commission of correction; members of the state industrial board; members of the public service and transit commissions; the commissioner of education; the commissioner of agriculture and markets; the commissioner of social welfare; the deputy of each officer specified in this subdivision; the secretary to the governor.

3. A member of congress or of the legislature or of any local legislative body.

4. A judge of a court of record, or not of record, or a surrogate.

5. A sheriff, under sheriff, or deputy sheriff regularly engaged in the performance of his duties.

6. The clerk or deputy clerk of any court.

No public officer or employee of the United States government, or of any state, city or municipality, or of any political subdivision of any of them or of any official board, authority, council, commission, corporation, or other agency of any of them, receiving annual compensation in excess of one thousand dollars from the aforesaid sources, shall serve on any grand jury.

§ 664–a. Challenge to the panel or array

It is not a good cause of challenge to the panel or array of trial jurors in an action in a court of record

1. that the officer who drew them is a party to, or interested in, the action, or related to a party; or

2. that they were notified to attend by an officer who is a party to, or interested in, the action, or related to a party, or is a resident of, or liable to pay taxes in, a city, village, town, or county which is a party to the action, unless it is alleged in the challenge, and established, that one or more of the jurors drawn were not notified and that the omission was intentional.

§ 665. Exemptions

Each of the following persons only, any inconsistent provision of law to the contrary notwithstanding, although qualified, is entitled to exemption from service as a juror upon claiming exemption therefrom:

1. A clergyman or minister of religion officiating as such and not following any other calling.

2. A practicing physician, surgeon, podiatrist, or dentist having patients requiring his daily professional attention, a licensed pharmacist actually engaged in his profession as a means of livelihood, a duly licensed embalmer actually engaged in his profession as a means of livelihood, and an optometrist actually engaged in the practice of optometry.

3. An attorney or counselor at law regularly engaged in the practice of law as a means of livelihood.

4. [See also subd. 4 below] A person belonging to the armed forces of the United States, and the active national guard and naval militia of the state.

4. [See also subd. 4 above] An active member of the army, air force, navy or marine corps of the United States, and the active national guard and naval militia of the state.

5. A member of a fire company or department or police force or department duly organized according to the laws of the state or any political subdivision thereof and performing his duties therein, or an exempt volunteer fireman, as defined in section two hundred of the general municipal law.

6. A captain, engineer, or other officer, actually employed upon a vessel making regular trips; or a licensed harbor or river pilot actually following that calling.

7. A woman.

8. An editor, editorial writer, a sub-editor, reporter or copy reader, actively and regularly employed in the handling or gathering of news for a daily, semi-weekly or weekly newspaper.

9. A person over seventy years of age.

§ 665–a. Ineligibility of jurors

The following persons shall be ineligible to serve as jurors: Any person who is knowingly a member of the communist party or any party or organization which advocates, advises or teaches the duty, necessity, desirability, or propriety of overthrowing or destroying the government of the United States, the government of any state, territory, district or possession thereof, or of any political subdivision therein, by force or violence, or who refuses to take the oath as provided by this law.

§ 666. Evidence of exemption

The evidence of the right to exemption as prescribed in section six hundred sixty-five is as follows: An affidavit of the applicant or of another person in his behalf, satisfactory to the commissioner, stating the facts entitling the applicant to exemption, or in the case of an exempt volunteer fireman, the certificate provided for in section two hundred two of the general municipal law.

Each affidavit must be filed with the commissioner and must be kept open by him at all reasonable times to public inspection.

The right to exemption must be claimed at the time of examination for liability to serve as a juror. If a person fails to present such claim at such time, he shall be deemed to have waived the same and cannot be exempted thereafter except for reasons accruing after the time of examination. If, however, he claims exemption at the time of his examination and is not granted the same, he may present such claim for exemption to the court when drawn for jury service or may review such refusal in the manner provided by article seventy-eight of the civil practice act.

§ 666–a. Compensation on waiver of exemption

Notwithstanding the provisions of any general, special or local law or charter provision, where a person entitled to claim an exemption from service as a juror is in the employ of any person, association, firm, corporation, partnership, political subdivision, government agency, or other public employer which by rule, ordinance or practice compensates employees who are required to perform jury service, such person, otherwise entitled to an exemption and who elects to waive that exemption and serve as a juror, shall be entitled to receive the same compensation from his employer as if he were required to serve as a juror.

§ 667. Notification of acceptance as juror

After a person has qualified satisfactorily as a juror, the commissioner may, in his discretion, issue a notice to such person, inform-

ing him that he has been found qualified to serve as a juror and
that he will be notified when he has been drawn for actual service.
The notice may also request such person to notify the commissioner
if he becomes entitled to exemption and claims such exemption or
becomes disqualified thereafter, and may also request him to inform
the commissioner of changes in address or occupation and of any
other information the commissioner may request.

§ 668. Preparation of ballot; general ballot box; electronic device

The commissioners shall prepare a ballot for each person as soon
as such person has qualified for jury service. The ballots must be
uniform and shall contain the name, occupation and address of the
juror and may also indicate the time of year when the juror would
prefer to serve and such other information as the commissioner
deems necessary.

The commissioner shall place the ballot for each person qualified
to serve as a juror in a box, to be known as the general ballot box,
or other device used in the drawing, from which shall be drawn all
trial jurors for the supreme court, the county court, the surrogate's
court and the district court. The general ballot box or other device
shall be retained in the office of the commissioner and shall be kept
securely locked and sealed except at the time of an authorized
drawing when it shall be opened under the supervision of the judge
and the sheriff in charge of the drawing, and after the drawing shall
be again sealed under the supervision of the judge and the sheriff.
The general ballot box shall be cylindrical in form with an aperture
large enough only to admit the hand of the person by whom the
ballots are to be drawn. The aperture shall be provided with a
cover so arranged as to be conveniently locked and sealed when
closed.

If the county employs an electronic device for drawing the names
of qualified trial jurors, the ballots shall be kept in locked file
cabinets of the type in conventional use for punched cards or
vaults or other protective housing suitable for the storage of
magnetic tape, perforated paper tape and cards or microfilm.

At the time of each authorized drawing the ballots made out
since the last drawing, as well as ballots of those persons who last

served at least two years previously and are therefore again liable for service, shall be placed in the general ballot box or other device after the drawing of jurors is completed, or during the course thereof if the box or other device becomes empty and before it is again sealed.

For local and inferior courts in a city or town, ballots shall be prepared by the commissioner and sent to the justices or clerks of the courts, or shall be prepared from the lists furnished by the commissioner to the town and city clerks pursuant to subdivisions four and five of section six hundred fifty-seven.

A commissioner of a county within the territory covered by the United States district court for the northern and western district of New York may open a ballot box or other device used in the drawing at the request in writing of a United States district judge to furnish names of qualified jurors for service in the United States courts for those districts.

§ 669. Drawing of trial jurors for the supreme court, county court, surrogate's court and district court

On a day designated by the commissioner, not less than fourteen nor more than twenty-eight days before the day appointed for holding a jury term of the supreme court, county court, surrogate's court and district court, the county judge and the sheriff, deputy sheriff or under sheriff, must attend at the office of the commissioner of jurors or any other room in the court house designated by the presiding judge, to supervise the proper drawing of jurors to attend at such term. The commissioner must notify the county judge and the sheriff in writing at least three days before the drawing.

In case of the absence of the county judge or in case of the failure of the county judge to attend at the time and place specified for the drawing, the commissioner may renotify him or may notify any other judge of a court of record residing or sitting in the county. When it is necessary to renotify the county judge or notify another judge of a court of record, such notification may be oral and a reasonable time shall be given.

The commissioner shall draw such number of jurors as he believes necessary and sufficient, unless otherwise prescribed by rule

of the justices of the appellate division or unless the judge or justice
appointed to hold the jury term shall otherwise direct.

§ 671. Mode of drawing

A drawing must be conducted publicly as follows:

1. The officer designated by law to perform the drawing must
shake or turn the receptacle containing the ballots so as to mix
them thoroughly, unless ballots are kept in locked file cabinets of
the type in conventional use for punched cards or vaults, or other
protective housing suitable for the storage of magnetic tape, perforated paper tape and cards or microfilm.

2. He must then, without seeing the name contained on any
ballot, publicly draw out of the ballot box one ballot at a time until
the requisite number has been drawn, or select such requisite
number by means of a punched card sorter or collator or an
electronic device employing mathematically programmed routines
for random selection.

3. In drawing ballots for the trial of a criminal action which is
or may be punishable by the infliction of the death penalty, if the
name of a person is drawn who has declared in his signed statement to the commissioner that he has conscientious scruples against
the death penalty which would prevent him from finding a verdict
of guilty of any crime punishable by death, the ballot containing
that person's name shall be set aside and returned to the ballot box
after completion of the drawing.

4. As each ballot is drawn, if notation has been made thereon,
consideration may, in the discretion of the commissioner or judge
supervising the drawing, be given to the time of year when the
juror shall prefer to serve. If the ballot is drawn of a person who
has expressed a preference for service at a time other than that
for which the drawing is being held and it is decided in the exercise of such discretion to postpone his service, the ballot containing
his name shall be set aside for summoning at the time of preference.
Not later than one month before the time of preference his ballot
shall be placed in a separate ballot box, pursuant to subdivision
two of section six hundred eighty-three.

5. As each ballot is drawn during a drawing for the supreme
court, county court, surrogate's court and the district court, it may

be checked against the index cards or questionnaires or any lists prepared by the commissioner.

If a ballot is drawn containing the name of a person who is shown by the records of the commissioner as not competent to serve by virtue of the provisions of section six hundred seventy-five, the ballot shall be removed from the general ballot box or other device from which such ballot is drawn and proper notation made on his record according to the month and the year when the person whose name appears on the ballot last served.

If during a drawing for the supreme court, county court, surrogate's court and the district court, a ballot is drawn containing the name of a person who is shown by the records of the commissioner to be no longer eligible, competent or qualified for jury service for cause accruing since his examination, other than set forth in the preceding paragraph of this subdivision, or to have been placed on the grand jury list, the commissioner shall forthwith destroy the ballot or may set it aside for further investigation for not more than two months, such ballot being marked with the reason for such disposition.

6. For courts other than the supreme court, county court, surrogate's court and the district court, if a ballot is drawn containing the name of a person no longer eligible or qualified for jury service for cause accruing since his examination or containing the name of a person who has been placed on the grand jury list, it shall be set aside and the minute required to be kept by subdivision seven below shall be marked accordingly.

7. A minute of the drawing must be kept by one of the attending officers, in which must be entered the name contained on each ballot drawn and the court for which it is drawn or any other disposition made pursuant to this article. The minute must be certified by the attending officers.

When the drawing is for jurors to serve in the supreme court, county court, surrogate's court and the district court, the minute thereof shall be filed in the commissioner's office. When the drawing is for jurors to serve in other courts, the minute shall be retained in the inferior local court for which the drawing was held until the conclusion of the service of the jurors and shall be sent to the office of the town or city clerk, or to the commissioner if the ballots or lists were received directly from his office together with the information required by sections six hundred eight-one and six hundred eighty-two.

8. When the drawing is completed, the ballot box or other device used in the drawing shall be closed and sealed in the presence of the attending officers, and shall not again be opened nor the seal broken until another drawing, except in pursuance of law. All the approved ballots drawn shall be delivered to the clerk, or if there is no clerk, to the judge of the court for which the jurors were drawn, for use during each term, session or trial, except where a central jury system is in operation.

9. In counties employing punched cards and punched card machines, or equipment employing coded input, magnetic tape, perforated paper tape and cards, or microfilm for the maintenance of jury records, locked file cabinets, of the type in conventional use for punched cards, vaults or other suitable protective housing, may be substituted for ballot boxes.

In counties employing punched cards and punched card machines, or equipment employing coded input, magnetic tape, perforated paper tape and cards, or microfilm for the maintenance of jury records, the drawing may be conducted by the use of a punched card sorter, a punched card collator, electronic devices employing mathematically programmed routines for random selection or by other mechanical means which will result in a drawing by lot.

The minute of the drawing may be prepared directly from the drawn ballots by a punched card accounting machine or equipment employing coded input, magnetic tape, perforated paper tape and cards, or microfilm.

§ 675. Length of service of jurors and limitation on recurrence thereof

A person who has served as a trial juror in any court within the state, including a federal court, shall not be competent to serve again as a trial juror in any court within the state, for two years subsequent to the last day of his service.

A person who has served as a grand juror in any court within the state, including a federal court, shall not be competent to serve again as a grand juror or as a trial juror in any court within the state for two years subsequent to the last day of his service.

Such service, unless otherwise specified by the justices of the appellate division, is hereby defined as:

(a) For trial jurors—not less than five days nor more than two weeks, Sundays and holidays excluded, except that such service shall continue beyond such period until the conclusion of any trial on which a trial juror may be engaged.

(b) For grand jurors—the sitting of the term of court for which a grand juror is drawn, unless sooner discharged, and except that if the grand jury sits less than five days, he may be required to serve another term.

Nothing contained in this section shall invalidate a verdict returned by a trial jury or an indictment returned by a grand jury, even though such trial or grand jury includes one or more trial or grand jurors respectively not compentent by virtue of such previous service.

§ 676. Notification of jurors for service

The commissioner must notify or direct the sheriff to notify each juror drawn for service in the supreme court, county court, surrogate's court and district court, by serving upon such juror notice to that effect and specifying the place where and the time when he is required to attend.

The notice may be served personally or by leaving it at the juror's residence or place of business or employment with a person of suitable age and discretion at least six days before the beginning of the term or the day for which the juror is drawn. The notice may also be served by mail if mailed at least nine days before the day appointed for such juror to appear, in which case said notice shall be enclosed in a securely closed postpaid wrapper, addressed to such juror at his residence or place of business or employment, and properly posted.

In courts other than the supreme court, county court, surrogate's court and district court, the officer designated by law shall notify jurors for service. The notice must be served at least three days before the day appointed for the juror to appear, in any of the ways set forth above.

Periods of notice shall not apply to the notification of additional jurors drawn as provided for in section six hundred seventy-four.

§ 678. Excuses and postponements

The judge of the trial court may, in his discretion, on the application of a trial juror, excuse him from a part or the whole of the time of service required of him as a juror or may postpone the time of service of a juror to a later day during the same or subsequent term of the court, or, by consent of such court, may postpone the time of service of a juror to a later date during the same or a subsequent term in any other court sitting within the county.

A person who has been notified to attend and who applies to be excused as prescribed in this section must present the notice to the judge. If he cannot personally attend he must send it by a person capable of making the necessary proof in relation to his claim to be excused or he may submit a request to be excused in writing accompanied by the necessary proof.

A note of the excuse and of the reason therefor, attested by the judge, who must append his signature or initials thereto, must be made or endorsed upon the notice to attend; or, if the person notified has not brought it into court, upon a separate sheet of paper which must be transmitted to the commissioner of jurors as a part of the report required by section six hundred eight-two.

§ 678–a. Excuses and postponements in a county using a central jury system

In any county using a central jury system for the impanelling of trial jurors for civil cases by court order for the supreme, county and surrogate's courts, the court, or the commissioner of jurors with the approval of the court, may postpone or excuse a trial juror when his interests, or those of the public may be materially injured by such service, or when he is a party in any action or proceeding to be tried or determined at any term for which he may have been summoned, or where his own health or the sickness or death of a member of his family requires his absence. The commissioner of jurors shall keep a record of each juror so postponed or excused and all records of attendance in connection with the central jury system.

§ 679. Discharge by the court

The court must discharge a person from serving as a trial or a grand juror in the following cases, where the causes justifying the discharge have arisen after examination for eligibility, or where the person claimed exemption at the time of examination and was refused:

1. Where it satisfactorily appears that he is not qualified.

2. Where it satisfactorily appears that he is disqualified.

3. Where it satisfactorily appears that he is exempt and he claims the benefit of the exemption.

Where a person is discharged for any of the causes specified in this section, the commissioner must destroy the ballot containing his name within sixty days after receiving notice of the juror's discharge.

§ 680. Trial jurors drawn for court to serve in other parts, terms or courts

A trial juror drawn for service in any court must serve as a trial juror in any other term or part of the same court when it sits in terms or parts, or, by consent of such court, in any other court sitting at the same time within the county. When so serving in such other term, part or court, his service shall be with the same power, force and effect as if he had been drawn as a trial juror for service in such other term, part or court.

§ 684. Grand jurors

1. Number and selection of grand jurors. The names of three hundred persons to serve as grand jurors at any term of the supreme court and county court, shall be selected annually for each county in the manner prescribed in this section for each year beginning January first and expiring December thirty-first following. Such number may, however, be changed by rule of the justices of the appellate divisions of the supreme court for any county embraced within their respective departments.

The annual grand jury list shall be selected by the commissioner in the manner specified in section six hundred seventy-one from the names of persons selected as qualified to serve as trial jurors, pursuant to section six hundred sixty-two, or in such other manner as may be prescribed by rule of the justices of the appellate division.

2. County jury boards. The county jury board shall meet annually at the office of the commissioner during the months of November or December on a date to be fixed by the chairman of the board. The supreme court justice shall act as chairman; in case of the absence of the supreme court justice, and in Albany and Westchester counties, the county judge shall act as chairman. Two of the members shall be necessary to constitute a quorum for the transaction of business, and if a quorum be not present the board shall adjourn from day to day until a quorum is obtained. The commissioner shall act as secretary of the board. The county board may further convene from time to time to fill any vacancies in the lists of grand jurors or to add such number of names thereto as are necessary.

3. Ballots; drawing of grand jurors. The commissioner shall prepare ballots for every name on the annual grand jury list in the same manner as for trial jurors and shall deposit them at the time of the first drawing after the annual selection of the grand jury list in a receptacle known as the grand jury ballot box, unless ballots are kept in locked file cabinets of the type in conventional use for punched cards or vaults or other protective housing suitable for the storage of magnetic tape, perforated paper tape and cards or microfilm, which shall be retained in the office of the commissioner and shall be kept securely locked and sealed except at the time of an authorized drawing. Notice of the time and place of the drawing shall be given by the commissioner to the judge supervising the drawing, the sheriff, and the clerk of the court for a term for which the grand jurors are being drawn.

The drawing of grand jurors shall be conducted at the same time and in the same manner as prescribed by law for drawing trial jurors for the supreme court and the county court, or at such other time as may be required by the court.

Unless otherwise provided in the case of the supreme court by an order made by a justice authorized to hold a term of such court, or in the case of the county court by a provision in the order direct-ing the drawing of the grand jury, there shall be drawn for each grand jury panel such number of grand jurors within the require-ments of law as the commissioner deems necessary. Where more than one grand jury is to be empaneled in a court on the same day, it shall not be necessary for the commissioner to draw separate groups of names for each grand jury panel.

A minute of such drawing shall be kept, signed and filed in the office of the commissioner in the same manner as for trial jurors.

4. Summoning of grand jurors. Grand jurors shall be summoned by the commissioner or the sheriff in the same manner as trial jurors are summoned for service in the supreme court and the county court.

5. Grand jurors; how drawn for actual service. The clerk of the court shall place in the wheel provided for that purpose, or other device used in the drawing, ballots provided by the commissioner, of persons drawn and summoned as grand jurors.

When but one grand jury is to be empaneled and more than twenty-three persons summoned as grand jurors attend for service and none are excused by the court, the clerk of the court shall openly draw out of the wheel, or other device used in the drawing, twenty-three ballots and the persons whose names are drawn con-stitute the grand jury.

When more than one grand jury panel is to be empaneled for the same court on the same day, the clerk of the court shall openly draw out of the wheel twenty-three ballots and the persons whose names are drawn shall constitute the first grand jury panel to be drawn. He shall then draw out of the wheel, or other device used in the drawing, twenty-three more ballots and the persons whose names are drawn shall constitute the second grand jury panel to be drawn. The names of the persons to constitute any additional grand jury panels shall be drawn in the same manner.

6. Additional grand jurors. If, at any term of a court for which a grand jury is to be empaneled, there shall not appear at least eighteen persons to serve as grand jurors, or if the number of grand jurors attending shall be reduced below eighteen before the grand jury is empaneled and sworn in, the court must, by order to be entered in its minutes, require the commissioner to draw and sum-

mon forthwith such additional number of grand jurors as shall be necessary, and must specify the number required in the order.

The drawing shall be held in the manner provided for regular grand jurors, except that notice thereof is not required.

The additional grand jurors shall be summoned in the manner required for grand jurors originally drawn.

No provisions in this article as to intervals of time with regard to the drawing, notification and attendance of jurors shall apply to additional grand jurors.

7. Report by court clerk after conclusion of service of grand jurors. After the adjournment of the term at which the grand jurors served, the trial court clerk shall report to the commissioner in the same manner as for trial jurors and the same proceedings shall be held subsequent to such report as for trial jurors except that the ballots of persons who appeared but were not drawn for actual service shall, unless otherwise directed by the court, be returned to the grand jury ballot box, or other device used in drawing.

8. Grand juries to sit concurrently. A grand jury may be empaneled at any term of the supreme court, and another in the county court, and may meet at and sit during the same time, but whenever either grand jury shall present an indictment against any person for any offense, it shall not be lawful for the other grand jury sitting at the same time to hear or act upon the same matter, or make any presentation in relation thereto, so far as it shall relate to the person so presented by the other grand jury.

Index

179